REACHING YOUTH
for CHRIST

by
TORREY JOHNSON

and
ROBERT COOK

MOODY PRESS
153 INSTITUTE PLACE
CHICAGO, ILLINOIS

Printed in the United States of America

PREFACE

It had to be done.

This book was a compulsion—Spirit-impelled.

Here's how it came about:

"Chicagoland Youth for Christ," as you will read in these pages, was launched amid fears and prayers—fears lest we had bitten off more than we could chew, and prayers of desperate longing that the rich blessing of God might be upon the venture.

Then . . . God worked, banishing our fears and answering our prayers so marvelously that the only possible reaction was a consuming desire to give Him all the glory. If only we could tell all the world how wonderfully God had met every need!

Co-incident with the apparent success of this child of faith, there came a flood of inquiries from people who wanted to start a similar ministry in their own towns and cities

"How did you get started?"

"How much does it cost?"

"Must we have a broadcast?"

"How did you get everybody to work with you?"

"Can you come over and help us get started?"

There we were, mired down in a flood of work ourselves, unable to give help to others—help they deserved, and help they needed if their work were to be launched profitably and successfully. If only we had some way of putting out some helpful suggestions to these inquiring folk—if only we could take off a few weeks and travel about helping others to get started! But we couldn't!

Then came Mr. Don Norman, of Moody Press, with a suggestion. How about a book on the "Youth for Christ" movement? Could we, would we, put such a book together?

Humbly we bowed and said, "Thank you, Lord, for hearing our heart's cry. We desire to give Thee all the glory, and to help others along the way of a successful ministry to young people."

And it is with this prayer that this book, "REACHING YOUTH FOR CHRIST," is sent forth.

TORREY JOHNSON
ROBERT COOK

CONTENTS

CHAPTER

1. How Things Begin - - - - - - 9
   The Spirit of God moved . . . .

2. Let's Keep It On A Miracle Basis! - - 15
   Is Anything Too Hard For The Lord?

3. Greater Than Our Faith - - - - - 20
   Able to do exceeding abundantly above all that we ask or think.

4. The Work Goes On - - - - - 25
   God also working with them.

5. "By My Spirit" - - - - - - - 31
   By My Spirit, saith the Lord.

6. Getting Started In Your Town - - - 35
   Every man in his place.

7. Radio: "The Lengthened Reach" - - - 44
   Witnesses . . . unto the uttermost part.

8. Messages God used in Winning Souls at Orchestra Hall - - - - - - 63
   My word . . . shall not return unto me void.

Illustrations between pages 32 and 33

INTRODUCTION

OF these last days it was prophesied long ago, "I will pour out of my Spirit upon all flesh: and your sons and your daughters shall prophesy, and your young men shall see visions" (Acts 2:17).

Today is distinctly a day of youth, in the roll of drums and the roar of battle, in the realm of government and the region of business, and especially in the religious light of America. Young people have found Jesus Christ as a sufficient Saviour from the penalty and power of sin, and with vision, enthusiasm and compassion are presenting Him to those who know Him not. Their faith is unbounded, their courage unafraid, their zeal unflagging; and their effectiveness is tremendous. They are crusaders for the Crucified, Risen, and Coming Christ.

REACHING YOUTH FOR CHRIST tells the story.

DR. V. RAYMOND EDMAN,
President of Wheaton College

CHAPTER ONE

HOW THINGS BEGIN

"HELLO! Doug? This is Torrey. Did I get you out of bed?"

"That's O K, Pal. What's on your heart?"

"We just had a prayer meeting and have come to our decision. We are ready to go ahead with 'Youth for Christ' in Chicago and want you to be free to begin to work two weeks from tomorrow, if you feel so led. How do you feel about it?"

"That's swell! You fellows know that I've been praying for something like this to happen for a long time, and I'll be ready—April 28."

After a little further conversation, the telephone receivers clicked on both ends of the line, and Doug Fisher—turning to his wife, Betty—shouted gleefully, " 'Youth for Christ' is going ahead, and I'm to begin two weeks from tomorrow."

That midnight call from Columbus, Ohio to Chicago on the evening of April 13, 1944 was the culmination of many months of prayer and thoughtful consideration as to the possibility of a "Youth for Christ" movement in Chicago. Among those who had been spending much time in prayer concerning this matter were Beverly Shea, formerly of New York City and then on the staff of the Moody Bible Institute; Lacy Hall, formerly with Glenn Wagner and his "Youth for Christ" movement in Washington, D. C.; Robert Cook of LaSalle, Illinois; Douglas Fisher of WMBI; William Erny of the Mid-West Church of the Air; and Torrey Johnson.

God used Beverly Shea. He and Jack Wyrtzen had worked in the same insurance office in New York City for about eight years and had been intimately associated in the work of the Lord throughout all that time. Beverly was with Jack when he started his "Word of Life" Hour and "Youth for Christ" meeting held at Times Square each Saturday night. He shared with Jack, Carlton Booth, and others the prayer and burdens of those early days. He had also been presented at rallies in the various parts of the country with Jack, and spent three months, June 15 to September 15, 1943, in continuous work in the interest of the "Word of Life" Hour.

Beverly had seen "Youth for Christ" in New York City grow from a small gathering into a movement large enough to pack Madison Square Garden with 20,000 people on April 1, 1944, with more than ten thousand turned away. He had seen hundreds won to the saving knowledge of the Lord Jesus Christ and had witnessed the radio development of the "Word of Life" Hour until it spread over more than twenty stations, and around the world by short wave.

When Shea first came to work for the Moody Bible Institute in Chicago, he became burdened for the same kind of youth work in Chicago as that carried on in New York. Often when we would meet or work together in meetings, he would say, "Torrey, there should be a 'Youth for Christ' meeting in Chicago every Saturday night. You're the man to get it started." Repeatedly we brushed him off with the remark that we had all we could do with a growing church, the work of the Mid-West Church of the Air, and other obligations that rested upon us. All the time, however, God kept speaking to our hearts, and we became increasingly burdened and interested. Often in secret prayer we would cry out, "O, God, if you want this work done and if you want us to do it, lead us definitely by Thy Holy Spirit."

God always answers such a prayer if it is presented in humility and in faith. Surely, regarding "Chicagoland Youth for Christ," He looked down with compassion and shaped the course of events so that finally there was no uncertainty in our hearts as to His will.

One day after Beverly Shea had returned from New York in the fall of 1942, he called and said, "There's a fellow who has just enrolled at the Moody Bible Institute, whom I would like you to meet. He has just come from Washington, D. C., where he was associated with Glenn Wagner in his 'Youth for Christ' movement in the nation's capital." Glenn Wagner was a former University of Illinois athlete in the days of "Red" Grange. God has graciously saved him and is mightily using him in Washington, D. C., to win many precious souls for the Lord Jesus Christ.

A few days later we met Lacy Hall. Again the same challenge came—this time it was from Lacy. He said, "Chicago ought to have a 'Youth for Christ' and while I have never met you before, Beverly says that you're the man God would have to get it started. Others have told me the same thing. I know what is going on in Washington and in New York, and I am sure that God would bless a similar effort in Chicago. Why don't you try it?"

We smiled again, shrugged our shoulders, and said, "But we have more than we can handle now. Surely someone else ought to get this thing under way. We will be glad to help in any way that we can."

When God wants you to do a job, however, He is not satisfied to have you pass it off on someone else. God is not looking for your *assistance*. He is looking for your *allegiance*. He wants a complete surrender of your entire will to Him. If He is calling you for a particular job, like Jonah of old, it is not easy to turn Him aside.

Such was God's call concerning "Chicagoland Youth for Christ." He was working, and He was answering prayer. He was using both men and circumstances to bring to pass His purpose. During 1943 we had the opportunity of speaking or participating in meetings for the "Voice of Christian Youth" in Detroit and in the newly begun "Youth for Christ" movement in Indianapolis, Indiana. In both of these meetings, God blessed and through these meetings, He spoke to our hearts. We knew the job could be done in Chicago and believed that God wanted the job done in Chicago, but we were hesitant to believe that we were chosen of the Lord for such a task as this.

The Spirit kept prompting, however, and dealing: "God wants YOU to get this job started."

"The Voice of Christian Youth" in Detroit is carried on by young men and young women who are occupied during the day with school and secular employment. God has marvelously blessed them throughout the years. In Indianapolis God used a young pastor of the Christian Missionary Alliance Church, Roger Malsbary, to get the work under way there. We preached at one of his opening rallies in June, 1943. It was a hot night, and there were about seven hundred present. After the meeting, on the way home to Chicago, we said, "Malsbary is sunk with a budget of more than six hundred dollars; he will never make the grade in the heat of July and August." But God rebuked our unbelief and during July and August, "Youth for Christ" in Indianapolis went forward increasingly and has flourished ever since.

God seemed to say, "If I can bless and use a young insurance clerk in New York, a former athlete in Washington, a group of young people not especially trained for Christian work in Detroit, and bring a young pastor from a nearby village into Indianapolis, don't you think I am sufficient for Chicago?" It was the old story that all of us know and yet few experience—it was that which the prophet was thinking when he said, "Not by might, nor by power, but by my spirit saith the Lord." It was Paul who said, "Not many mighty—but God hath chosen the foolish things of the world to confound the wise."

During Founder's Week Conference in February 1944, we received a telephone call from Richard Harvey, pastor of the Christian Missionary Alliance Church of St. Louis. He was in Chicago not only for Moody Bible Institute's annual conference, but also to contact speakers for his

"Youth for Christ" in St. Louis—a work which was to begin in March. Harvey called us and asked whether we'd come. We said we would. After having accepted his invitation, we said, "Dick, come over and speak at our prayer meeting on Wednesday, and tell us more about your 'Youth for Christ' movement." He came.

After the prayer meeting, we ate together in the railroad station while waiting for his train. When we had finished, we said, "Tell us now, Dick, all about your plans for St. Louis."

"Well," he replied, "I am sinking everything that I have into it. I have only been in St. Louis for a short while, and I have a very small congregation. If 'Greater St. Louis Youth for Christ' fails, people will lose confidence in me, and I will have to start somewhere else, but I can't get away from this thing. God wants this youth movement for St. Louis. I have laid the whole matter out before Mrs. Harvey; she is with me, and we are putting every cent that we have into the venture. We have rented Kiel Auditorium, the civic auditorium of St. Louis. It has three halls, one seating seven hundred, one four thousand, and the large one seating fifteen thousand, and we will not be satisfied until the largest one is filled."

"What's your budget for this program, Dick?"

"It will cost conservatively about six hundred dollars each week, and everyone participating is donating his services, including myself."

It was about time now for Dick to board the train, and after having bid him "good-bye," as we were returning to our car, we said, "Surely hope he makes it. It's a big load, but he has great faith."

Two months passed by, and from April 12 to 17, the National Association of Evangelicals held their annual conference in Columbus, Ohio. We were there. One day we saw Dick Harvey on the conference floor and inquired, "How is the 'Greater St. Louis Youth for Christ' movement going?"

"Wonderful!" was his reply. "The crowds are running

well over two thousand and souls are being saved and every need is being met."

"Dick, come over to our hotel room and tell us more about it. We're interested."

He came. We sat down and he explained all the details of God's working in St. Louis. All the time Dick was giving his account, the Spirit of God was saying, "It's working in New York City. God is blessing in Washington. It's going in Detroit. Souls are being saved in Indianapolis. Now Dick Harvey, a comparative stranger to that city, has been blessed of the Lord in St. Louis. Can you not trust God to meet your need in Chicago?" Looking up into His face, we said, "Yes, by the grace of God, we will." That night after prayer, at the midnight hour, a long distance call was put in for Doug Fisher, and "Chicagoland Youth for Christ" was launched.

CHAPTER TWO

LET'S KEEP IT ON A MIRACLE BASIS

O GOD, we want this kept on a miracle basis. We want everyone to know that God's hand is on this movement. We want folks to see that this is too big and too great for any man or group of men to accomplish by themselves. We want folks to say, 'GOD DID IT!' "

When we had finished our season of prayer, Bob Cook repeated, "Let's keep this thing on a miracle basis from beginning to end all the way through." "Amen, Brother!" chimed in the rest of those who had been praying, as they contemplated securing a hall for "Chicagoland Youth for Christ," a radio outlet, the financial support, and the backing of interested young people and business men.

God had seemed to bring the original group of workers together miraculously. He had brought Beverly Shea from New York City to the Moody Bible Institute where his favor and influence had grown by leaps and bounds. He had led Douglas Fisher by a round-about way from Toronto's Canadian Broadcasting Company to Chicago. Doug had for some time been in evangelistic work with Douglas Roe and now was on the staff of WMBI. Lacy Hall came to us by the Holy Spirit all the way from Washington, D. C. Robert Cook, who had been editor of the magazine, "Young People Today" and a youth leader, both in Philadelphia as well as in the Middle West; also Robert Wyatt, Floyd Gephart, and Bill Erny—all these men had been miraculously brought together with Torrey Johnson in the early days of planning and preparation for "Chicagoland Youth for Christ."

Who could say anything else but that this was of the Lord? Surely bringing men from Toronto, New York, Washington, and LaSalle, as well as Chicago, and equipping those men with talents that dove-tailed so well, could have been the work of none but the Holy Spirit.

We say, then, this was a miracle of God.

The prospect of a meeting place for "Chicagoland Youth for Christ," as the work began, was very discouraging. Some wanted a hall that was acoustically perfect in order to produce the best program possible. Others wanted a theatre building where the unsaved would be willing to come. No one even dreamed of the possibility of Orchestra Hall, acoustically the most perfect auditorium in Chicago, centrally located, and a place where both saved and unsaved gather upon different occasions—but God is abundantly greater than both our fears and our faith.

The only other suitable auditorium in down-town Chicago seated but five hundred people, and the theaters of Chicago, with the Republican and Democratic Conventions going on, were not going to close for the summer of 1944. The situation looked very discouraging on Saturday, April 29. The opening date of "Chicagoland Youth for Christ," May 27, was only four weeks away, and there was as yet—no auditorium!

Having to leave the office for some hours in the early afternoon on that never-to-be-forgotten April Saturday, we turned to Einar Christianssen and said, "Einar, there is the telephone. Call up anywhere you can and see what you can find out about an auditorium. We seem to be getting nowhere." After several hours, we returned to the office. There were seated Douglas Fisher, Bob Cook, and Einar Christianssen. They all chimed in together saying, "We've got the place! It's Orchestra Hall—twenty-one weeks for five thousand dollars." We replied, "You fellows are crazy. Orchestra Hall seats three thousand, and we want a place seating about one thousand, and five thousand dollars—who is going to pay for it? We haven't a dime between us!"

At the same time we heard the still small voice of the Holy Spirit saying, "Is anything too hard for the Lord?" We replied, "No, nothing is too hard for Him."

That same evening we had dinner with "Pop" Cook, Bob's father. During the course of our conversation we said, "Look, Pop, if there were one wealthy man behind this work, there would be nothing to worry about, but five thousand dollars for an auditorium, the cost of a radio broadcast, the advertising, the help, and all the other expenses—who is going to pay them?" Mr. Cook replied, "If you had a millionaire behind you, you would be happy, but you have more than a millionaire, you have God! I think you fellows need to determine first whether God wants this job done, and then whether He wants you to do it. If you feel that God wants the job done and that He wants you to do it, you have nothing to worry about. He will see you through and meet your every need."

The following Monday morning we signed the contract for twenty-one weeks in Orchestra Hall, seating three thousand people. We had wanted a place for one thousand. Would God fill *this place?* He did, and we say that the securing of Orchestra Hall as the place where "Chicagoland Youth for Christ" began was a miracle of God's grace and power, far beyond the faith or plan of any one man or group of men.

Having now personnel and a hall, the next thing that we felt to be needful was a radio broadcast. How to get one—that was the question.

Newspapers and magazines, because of the paper shortage, had to cut down on advertising, and this drove many who would otherwise advertise in print to use the radio. Business everywhere was picking up and more money was being spent on radio advertising than ever before. More than that, many station owners did not want the gospel on the air.

We tried every major station in Chicago and were met with the same answer, "We already have more religion on the air than we want. In the future we expect to cut off some that we now have. There is no place for you." The situation seemed quite hopeless, but we wanted to be "geared to the times and anchored to the Rock." How could we be "geared to the times" without a broadcast? Jack Wyrtzen had one; Roger Malsbary had one; Dick Harvey in St. Louis had one, and we felt that we also needed the lengthened reach that only radio can give.

About this time Beverly Shea was to start his program, "Hymns from the Chapel," over the Blue Network station, WCFL, under the sponsorship of Club Aluminum Corporation—a great business with a consecrated Christian president, Herbert J. Taylor. We felt led of the Holy Spirit to speak to Mr. Taylor about our problem and solicit his help. God again marvelously undertook and, through the gracious co-operation of Mr. Taylor, we were able to secure one half hour on the Voice of Labor Station, WCFL . . . *after* we had already been turned down by that station on six previous occasions! "Chicagoland Youth for Christ" is the only Saturday evening gospel broadcast in Chicago. Again we lifted our hearts and said, "This is of the Lord. This is another miracle from above." God had now undertaken to bring together the personnel, to provide Chicago's finest Loop auditorium, and time on a very valuable network station.

We were ready now to present the work to Christian business men for their consideration and to outstanding youth leaders for their co-operation. Two banquets were held, the first for a group of about fifty business men, and the second for a group of about fifty Chicago young people's leaders. At both these banquets, we outlined to these friends, God's gracious dealings thus far, and how the Holy Spirit seemed to bring together these men for this job at this particular time. We wanted the favor of these influential people, but scarcely knew what their reaction would be. How little we sometimes trust the Lord!

No suggestion of any kind was made regarding financial support or any other obligation that these leaders might assume. We wanted their prayers and their good-will. God gave us that and more. At the close of each banquet, these business men and young people's leaders volunteered their prayerful co-operation, influence and support. In addition they also suggested that they wanted a part immediately underwriting some of the expenses of "Chicagoland Youth for Christ." It was thought that the first twenty-one weeks would cost about fifteen thousand dollars (since that time it has proved to cost even more than that) and these gracious Christian business men and leaders of young people's organizations kindly volunteered to support the work to the extent of more than three thousand dollars.

We could hardly keep back the tears as we thought of how wonderfully the Lord was working. "He which hath begun a good work . . . will perform it," and He who had begun "Chicagoland Youth for Christ" in the preparation of many hearts in different places was now bringing to pass the development of the program, and the time was approaching for the first meeting in Orchestra Hall. The personnel was ready; the hall had been secured; radio time had been contracted for; the backing of business and youth leaders and the good-will of pastors had been solicited.

Now . . . was God going to meet the challenge of filling an auditorium three times as large as we had at first contemplated? That is the story of Chapter Three.

GREATER THAN OUR FAITH

EVERYONE is alive to the problem of delinquency. There is delinquency among parents. There is delinquency among youth. The fact is that our whole nation has been negligent, disobedient and delinquent for many years. The tragedy is that very few know how to cope with this growing menace. One prominent social worker described the pitiable attempt at meeting the delinquency problem by saying, "There is nothing that we can do about a delinquent until after the case is brought into court."

Every true child of God says and repeats a thousand times over, "There are a multitude of things that can be done before a child is brought into court, and there are a multitude of things which, if done, will keep that child from ever getting into court." Thank God, "the gospel of Christ . . . is the power of God unto salvation to everyone that believeth."

Our hope from the very beginning of "Chicagoland Youth for Christ" was to help meet the challenge of a day of constantly increasing sinfulness. We believed with all our hearts that God was leading in this matter and were leaving no stone unturned, either by advertising, by the arrangement of an attractive musical program, or by the preparation of ushers, personal counselors, and speakers, to present God's very best to Chicago's youth.

Busy days—those four weeks between April 28, 1944, when Doug Fisher began working full time for "Chicagoland Youth for Christ" and Saturday, May 27, when the opening rally was held in Orchestra Hall. During that time the type of program to be followed had to be well thought out and prepared. The advertising material had to be printed and circulated throughout the city; help had to be secured for the usher band, for the personal workers, and for the All Girl Choir; and the entire personnel had to be thoroughly trained for their part in the work.

During those four weeks of final preparation, much prayer was going up, and prayer meetings were permitted to interrupt the work whenever anyone felt so led. The constant cry of every heart unto the Lord was, "O God, our supreme desire is that Thou mightest be glorified to the salvation of many, many precious souls."

Yes, we dared to ask God to give us in twenty-one weeks of the summer season, one thousand souls for Christ. We also cried out unto the Lord, "O, God, if it pleases Thee, fill Orchestra Hall!" Then, too, there was the financial load, and we had laughingly said, "If this thing fails, you friends will have to make pastoral calls on us in jail." The financial responsibility, however, was more than a bit of humor. It was something that would have to be met, and we prayed that God would meet the financial need each week, just as He provided manna for the children of Israel while they journeyed through the wilderness country.

We prayed that, from the beginning to the end, each program might be definitely under the guidance of the Holy Spirit. We prayed that each speaker, each musician, each testimony might present only a God-given message. In the midst of all our prayers we were glad that "the Spirit itself maketh intercession for us" because we found often that "we know not what we should pray for as we ought."

The work of promotion and advertising for "Chicagoland Youth for Christ" was placed in the hands of Robert Cook. His was the task of preparing the publicity so that insofar as our means would allow, everyone would know about "Chicagoland Youth for Christ." Those who appreciate the presentation of the printed page in the best form have said that Bob has "geared his advertising to the times, but has anchored the message to the Rock."

The music, with responsibility for what is called "good

production," was assigned to Douglas Fisher and Beverly Shea. They immediately secured two grand pianos for use with the four-manual concert organ of Orchestra Hall. What a musical team! There would be Douglas Fisher at the console of the organ; LaVerne Christiansen, an accomplished pianist and well acquainted with evangelistic work; and Blanchard Leightner of Radio Station WMBI. Fisher also had the responsibility of organizing the All Girl Choir; and Shea, in addition to his solo work, was given the radio "commercial," introducing and closing the broadcast. Robert Cook assumed the task of leading congregational singing. With this nucleus, and with the added help of scores of talented young people, the musical program "sparked" from the very beginning.

The "mechanics" of a service are important and God gave us the right folk to make the wheels go 'round. Lacy Hall, with a background of experience in "Youth for Christ" at Washington, D. C., organized a band of young ladies to do the work of ushering. Floyd Gephart, with his wide experience of handling personal workers at the Chicago Easter Sunrise Service each year, rallied together an efficient corps of personal workers, whom we call "Counselors." Robert Wyatt took charge of circulating advertising material, and William Erny, with a rich background of business experience as a manufacturer, negotiated the contracts. In addition to these already mentioned, there were also scores of others, both on the committee of recommendation and otherwise, who lent a ready and willing hand during that busy month of preparation preceding the opening rally on Saturday, May 27.

The responsibility commissioned to Torrey Johnson was to organize the various committees into units and to take charge of the rally from week to week. The meetings would be evangelistic throughout. They must be slanted directly toward youth. There must be life in the program, and yet it must be spiritual. There must be spontaneity, yet dignity. There must be liberty, yet the program must be on the highest possible level. Our aim was to present the gospel in as attractive a form as anything presented by the world.

We hoped, as a friend stated after one of the rallies, that young people would say, "The quality of this program is as good as anything the world has to offer." At the same time, we were also praying that there would be *conviction* and as a result, salvation, consecration and revival in all of these meetings.

Throughout the days of that month preceding the opening rally of Chicagoland, doubts often came to our minds, "Orchestra Hall is too large. You wanted a place seating one thousand. Now you have one seating three thousand. It will never be filled. Summer is coming on, and the vacation season is also at hand. You will never make the grade." The die was already cast, however, and so we had to look up continually and say, "O, God, increase our faith! O, God, do more than we ask or even think! O, God, in the name of Christ, we pray for at least one thousand souls to be won this summer season!"

Finally, May 27 arrived. It was the day toward which God had been planning and preparing our hearts. He had called together a group from various parts of America. He had raised up scores of fellow-helpers. He was now about to answer the prayers that had gone up from hundreds of hearts, many of whom we shall never know until we stand in the Presence of Christ. It was the day of our opening rally. Could God, would God, give us a gracious start in "Chicagoland Youth for Christ"? We didn't know. We scarcely dared to hope. We felt something like one of old who said, "Lord, I believe. Help Thou my unbelief."

The last thing that was done before the beginning of the meeting was to hold one further prayer huddle in the West Room of the basement of Orchestra Hall. Once more, those who were most interested, gathered together and cried unto the Lord. Present in that group were a large number of our committee of recommendation and other interested friends.

Finally the big moment came. Who would lead the

way up to the platform of Orchestra Hall? Who would dare to look in and give the rest of us a report as to the crowd? We hoped that the main floor seating one thousand would be filled and that no one would look up into the balconies and see the empty chairs. We do not remember who did go out on the platform first, but we know that before we went, *God was there*.

That evening for the opening rally God sent more than two thousand. Billy Graham, pastor of the Village Church of Western Springs, was the speaker. At the close of the meeting, more than forty hands were lifted, indicating a desire to accept the Lord Jesus Christ as their personal Saviour. When the offering was received, God had sent in enough to take care of the expenses of the following Saturday.

And then, suddenly, the meeting was over. We wept, shouted, and praised the Lord. He had given us an audience twice as large as our original expectation. He had given us more than two score souls for Christ, and expenses for the following week were met. "Chicagoland Youth for Christ" was now on the way with twenty weeks yet in Orchestra Hall. After that, what might our God yet have in store?

CHAPTER FOUR

THE WORK GOES ON

I HOPE we have as many as seven or eight hundred next Saturday. It would be too bad if we should fall very far below that mark on the second week," said Jim.

"What do you mean—seven hundred?"

"Well, after a big opening night with all the publicity and prayer and emphasis put upon it, we are bound to fall back—I hope not so far as to make it too discouraging for the future of the work."

That doubt seemed to be in many minds as we looked forward to the second "Chicagoland Youth for Christ "rally in Orchestra Hall. After all, maybe it wasn't too much in expect, that with all the effort put forth for the opening night and the curiosity of many who might attend once, there should be more than two thousand present. The second and third weeks were felt to be the acid test as to whether God was in this program or whether it was just a flash to die out as quickly as it arose.

You may be sure that much prayer went up throughout the days of that second week. We cried unto the Lord day by day privately, and in smaller and larger groups as well: "O, God, rebuke our unbelief, rebuke what otherwise might be the ridicule of the enemy, and give to us Thy blessings for the second meeting."

The speaker for the second rally was Dr. Peter Rees Joshua, Pastor of the First Presbyterian Church of Aurora, Illinois, and a Captain in the British Army in World War I. In music the program was well planned, and all was in readiness. After a season of prayer in the basement room of Orchestra Hall, it was time to approach the platform and begin the second meeting.

Once again, fear and anxiety mingled with faith gripped our hearts as we contemplated what the crowd might be. Who was first on the platform, we do not remember. But again we found that *God was there* before any of us arrived. When we lifted our eyes slowly from the main floor to the balcony, our hearts rejoiced to see more than two thousand gathered again for the second evening. At the close of the meeting a large response to the offer of salvation, and once again when the offering was received, there was just sufficient to carry on for the third rally of the following week. God had once more proved Himself faithful.

No sooner was the second meeting over and our thoughts directed toward the third meeting, but the same doubts crept in once again—"The people will get tired of this program. They will not stick to it week after week throughout the summer, and you will find a slump coming one of these times." All we could do was to pray and with our prayers seek the guidance of God. We can testify now that, as we labored and prayed, God continued to work with us and to pour out His blessings.

The attendance throughout the summer in Orchestra Hall has continuously exceeded two thousand, and the rallies have been averaging about twenty-five hundred each week. On numerous occasions Orchestra Hall has been filled and hundreds have been turned away. On the Saturday before Labor Day, every available corner was occupied and one thousand were estimated to have been turned away from the service. In all of these meetings scores of young people have been won to a saving knowledge of the Lord Jesus Christ and hundreds have been encouraged and inspired to go forth and serve Christ as never before.

On one particular Saturday in the middle of the summer two Navajo Indian boys came into the meeting and surrendered completely to Christ. A Japanese girl, who supposed that when she was baptized she became a Christian, saw her need of Christ and accepted Him as her

Saviour; a young sailor and his wife from Kokomo, Indiana, who had been backsliders, were restored to Jesus Christ, and a large company of civilian young fellows and girls, as well as servicemen, gave their hearts to Jesus Christ.

A Sunday school teacher had a class of ten boys, all of whom lived in a home for children of delinquents and unfortunates. Four of these boys had been professing Christians but six were unsaved. As a result of attending "Chicagoland Youth for Christ," on two successive Saturday nights, all ten came out and out for the Lord Jesus Christ, four to be restored and six others to accept Him as their personal Saviour. What a joy to realize that these who have had such a handicap at the start of life should now be given an opportunity to accept the Lord Jesus Christ!

A nurse had been a Christian but one evening, in response to the message, stepped out and yielded herself completely to the Lord Jesus Christ. The result is that in her hospital and among her friends, she has now organized a class for instruction in soul-winning. These young people are going forth and winning others to Him.

"That was the greatest experience of my entire life!" said one of the young lady ushers at the close of a meeting, after she had spoken with an elderly woman and led her to a saving knowledge of the Lord Jesus Christ. Yes, "Chicagoland Youth for Christ" has done a great deal for these girls who usher from week to week. They not only usher but also help in bringing souls to the Cross.

One evening a sailor responded to the invitation at the close of the meeting, and when asked how it was that he came to "Chicagoland Youth for Christ" rally replied, "Someone gave me a tract and told me that this was a good place. Believe me, they didn't tell half the truth. It's more than a good place. It's the best place on earth." That sailor that night met another fellow from the place where he was stationed, and he continued from that time to attend the meetings, together with the Christian friend that he had met in Orchestra Hall. What a joy to work with parents and loved ones of these in the Service, to bring their own to Christ!

On another occasion, a young man came forward to surrender for full time Christian work. After he had been dealt with and had filled out a card, giving us his name and address, so that we might keep in touch with him, we said, "Aren't you the son of an evangelist?"

"Yes," he replied, "I am, and my Dad is here tonight."

In a few minutes father met son—what a joyful meeting that was, as the father in full time Christian work welcomed his boy to the joyful fellowship of service for our Lord Jesus Christ.

One day a call came into the office. "I have to see Torrey Johnson. I am not saved. I have been under conviction since last Saturday, and I can't sleep. I'll go crazy if I am not saved soon." An appointment was made for the girl to see Torrey Johnson, but he was not able to keep the appointment. Without telling those in the office what was on her heart, she went on her way, even more sorrowfully than when she came.

She called again the next day.

"This thing is getting worse and worse. I am *so* under conviction! I have thought I was a Christian, but after last Saturday, I know I am not. I have to be saved."

"Won't you talk with Bob Cook? I know he will be very happy to help you," said the young lady who answered the telephone.

"Yes, I will. I will talk with anyone that can help me."

Over the telephone that day, Robert Cook led the fifteen-year-old girl to a saving knowledge of our Lord and Saviour, Jesus Christ.

These stories could be repeated in dozens of instances. Souls have been saved. Back-sliders have been reclaimed. Christian young people have dedicated their lives for full time Christian work. Others have come out into a clear-cut testimony and separation from the world. Of the fruit of this labor, it is impossible to tell fully. One pastor said,

" 'Youth for Christ' has meant more to my church and young people than anything else I could speak of. Our whole Sunday is transformed because our young people have attended 'Youth for Christ' on Saturday nights."

The encouragement given by "Chicagoland Youth for Christ" together with other Youth for Christ movements have stimulated the development of similar testimonies all over America. Inquiries have come to "Chicagoland Youth for Christ" from Tampa and Miami, Florida; Atlanta, Ga.; Augusta, Ga.; Columbus, Ohio; Toledo, Ohio; LaCrosse, Milwaukee, Kenosha, and Racine, Wisconsin; Rockford, Belvidere, and Chicago Heights, Illinois; Gary, Indiana; Sunnyside, Washington; Los Angeles, California; and even from as far away as Hamilton, Bermuda, where two Chicago sailor lads have started a "Youth for Christ" in the city hall! We can only pray and hope that this may be one channel, under God, of bringing about revival in these days.

The question is often asked, "What about the future of 'Youth for Christ,' both in Chicago and elsewhere?" This is a difficult question to answer. We can only reply, "It seems quite evident that God is in this movement."

If "Youth for Christ" took root in only one or two places, it could be attributed to unusual leadership or to especially providential circumstances. But "Youth for Christ" has taken root all over America, wherever it has been prayerfully and carefully launched. For that reason it seems evident that this movement is of the Lord and as long as He sees fit, it will continue.

In that spirit of faith, "Chicagoland Youth for Christ" presses on, trusting Him for guidance week by week. He who began the work by His Holy Spirit and raised up every provision will lead on so long as it suits His purpose.

The leaders of "Chicagoland Youth for Christ" felt that a fitting climax to the twenty-one weeks in Orchestra Hall would be a Victory Rally. Where could it be held? Where *should* it be held? The largest indoor stadium in America is the Chicago Stadium, seating upwards of twenty thousand people. Here have been held the Republican and Democratic National Conventions of 1944. What a place to have a "Youth for Christ" Victory Rally! What a testimony it might be to the entire nation, whose eyes have been focused upon that building and the candidates there selected to run for President of the United States.

Would the Chicago Stadium be open for that evening? Would those in authority rent it to "Youth for Christ"? The answer to both questions was "YES!" At this writing prayerful planning is being made for this rally in anticipation of a packed auditorium with multiplied thousands listening over the air and hundreds won to a saving knowledge of the Lord Jesus Christ. For the Victory Rally, T. J. Bittikofer has been selected to direct the 2,500 voice Youth Choir, and the Salvation Army is to provide a band, representative of all their corps in the Chicago area. In addition the support and encouragement of hundreds of churches and pastors in Chicago, as well as Bible-loving schools and colleges, have been given.

Growing out of the Chicago Stadium Rally will be the winter work of "Chicagoland Youth for Christ." The center of winter activities will be world-famous Moody Memorial Church, whose founder, D. L. Moody, was mightily used of God in bringing revival during the last half of the nineteenth century. Will God again awaken the spirit of D. L. Moody and move in Chicago, beyond Chicago, and throughout the length and breadth of America, to the salvation of another generation? Let us pray to that end!

The Moody Memorial Church seats four thousand people, and we are trusting that it will be filled every Saturday and that multiplied hundreds will be won to Christ throughout the coming winter. In the Spring—back to Orchestra Hall for the summer to follow and then . . . "the Spirit knoweth where it listeth and thou hearest the sound thereof and canst not tell whence it cometh or whither it goeth . . ."

We purpose to follow the Spirit of God.

CHAPTER FIVE

"BY MY SPIRIT"

THERE is a great deal of difference between a composite scene and a true pictorial. The one is made up of several pictures mounted together and then photographed—always artificial. The other, showing some impressive sweep of nature's handiwork, includes several possible "scenes"—but merges them all into one refreshing, harmonious whole.

Human reporting, because it *is* human, necessarily shares the musty flavor of the composite. But one has the feeling that if we were to view the "Youth for Christ" movement as God sees it, there would emerge the unified beauty of a great, sweeping horizon, on which God is working in several places at the same time.

Actually, the "Youth for Christ" movement has sprung up spontaneously throughout the United States. Times differ, as do methods and personnel structures, but underlying the entire movement is the unmistakable sign of God's handiwork. "Not by might, nor by power, but by my spirit, saith the Lord."

Take the matter of origins, for instance. All of the vigorous youth ministries we see today started with a conviction in the heart of a man—a conviction that God wanted something done.

Jack Wyrtzen, insurance company employee by day, preacher by night, would stand in Times Square on a Saturday night, his heart bleeding for the thousands there —unsaved and unreached. When he prayed for them, there came the conviction that God wanted him to do something about it. Out of that vision in the 1930's grew the great work of today, which has for more than three years weekly packed the Gospel Tabernacle auditorium at 8th Avenue and 44th Street in Times Square, New York City, broadcasting over more than a score of radio stations here and abroad, gospel messages slanted for young people.

Roger Malsbary, college-town preacher just outside of Indianapolis, felt a burden for the hundreds of young people within his reach, and yet unreached by the churches. Earnest prayer, the enlisting of cooperation from interested individuals, and the "Youth for Christ" movement was launched May 27, 1943 at the English Theater in Indianapolis. Interest has remained at a high peak, and God has blessed that venture since its inception. But again, God spoke to a man.

Glenn Wagner, former All-American football star, and now president of the Washington Bible Institute in Washington, D. C., felt a burden for the thousands of service men and the other young folk who throng the streets of our nation's capital. Growing out of this exercise of heart, there came the "Christian Youth and Service Men's Campaign." Saturday night youth rallies were the backbone of the work, with a radio broadcast, a free canteen for service men and women, and a program that would gain and hold the interest of young folk. The work goes on, with two full years of blessing behind them, and a future bright with the promises of the Lord. God found Glenn Wagner, a man who would listen to Him.

It was the same in St. Louis. Richard Harvey, pastor of the Christian and Missionary Alliance Church there, became burdened over the condition of young people in his city. Harvey, now in his thirties, had come to St. Louis to find a city packed with worldly amusements, but with no place where Christian young people could go for fellowship and service. Fervent prayer only served to increase the conviction that God had something for him to do.

A few "feeler" meetings with influential Christians finally resulted in a nucleus of a half-dozen conscientious Christian men, and the movement was on. A constitution

John Huffman, director of Boston "Youth for Christ."

Torrey Johnson, director of "Chicago-land Youth for Christ."

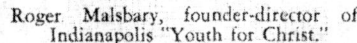

Roger Malsbary, founder-director of Indianapolis "Youth for Christ."

Jack Wyrtzen, dynamic leader of the New York group.

Jack Wyrtzen, director of "Word of Life" Hour and New York "Youth for Christ."

Glenn Wagner, former All-American football star, now directs a thriving youth program in Washington. D. C.

Johnson: "Let's put the punch in it!" Doug Fisher, Rose Arzoomanian, Beverly Shea and Bob Cook seem to be in agreement.

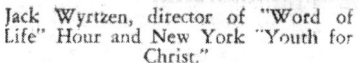

Part of the crowd of five thousand that gathered for Boston's initial "Youth for Christ" rally.

Full house at Orchestra Hall — a weekly miracle of God's grace!

Walter H Smyth, director of Philadelphia
Youth Center.

Song leader Bob Cook reaches for a
high note on his trombone.

Philadelphia Youth Center with Walter H. Smyth

Richard Harvey, director of St. Louis "Youth for Christ."

Radio Bible Quiz—a highlight of the St. Louis youth rallies. Richard Harvey in the pulpit.

Servicemen are ushers at Kiel Hall in the St. Louis "Youth for Christ" rallies.

Hatch Memorial Shell on Boston's Esplanade—scene of Boston's first "Youth for Christ" rally.

Carlton Booth, soloist of Jack Wyrtzen's "Word of Life" Hour.

Youth For Christ — the American flag. Young Americans are finding that patriotism and the gospel go well together

Posters, circulars and mailing cards were distributed to pastors
churches and key youth centers.

Ads in leading newspapers carried a 'different' kind of appeal
to attract attention

was drawn, committees on prayer, finance, publicity, etc., were appointed, and on February 26, 1944, there were more than 1,000 persons in the Municipal Auditorium for the first "St. Louis Youth for Christ" rally! God "sought for a man among them" in St. Louis, and He found Dick Harvey.

So it goes throughout the movement. There was Oscar Gillan in Detroit, back in 1938, first founder and director of the "Voice of Christian Youth," succeeded today by the vigorous leadership of Edward Darling, and his competent staff. There was Theodore Elsner, whose Philadelphia Youth Center started eleven years ago with fourteen young people gathered in a back room of his church on a Saturday night. Today Walt Smyth packs in 750 to 1,000 each week with a live-wire program. And in April of '44 there was Torrey Johnson, who said, "Lord, I believe you want me to start this thing. I don't know where the staff or the place or the program or the money are coming from, but I'll trust you for it all." George Wilson, with his staff, has found that thousands in Minneapolis were ready for "Youth for Christ," too.

Even as late as September 9, 1944, "Youth for Christ" started in Boston, with an estimated 5,000 on the esplanade in front of Hatch Memorial Shell. Moving later into Dr. Harold Ockenga's Park Street Church, the meeting filled the auditorium to capacity. John Huffman, director of the movement, announced that hundreds who had come out to hear Carlton Booth and Dr. Howard Ferrin were turned away.

God has been working among young people, wherever He could find a man who would listen!

Methods are strikingly similar. Over all, the list would be something like this:

A co-operative approach

Testimonies from two or three born-again Christians

A radio broadcast in connection with the service

Good music—the best available

A definite gospel invitation.

Innovations growing out of this basic technique depend upon the personality of the leaders. Dick Harvey has a radio quiz for St. Louis boys and girls. Glenn Wagner has a free canteen for service men, set up each Saturday night prior to the meetings. The Detroit "Voice of Christian Youth" features annual boat cruises on Lake St. Clair, banquets, and a Gospel Team ministry. Interesting advertising angle is their Sales Promotion Group, with district managers in the various churches, serving under a regional manager, who in turn reports directly to the promotional chairman. Mailing groups, prayer groups, and personal workers are all handled under volunteer leadership. Philadelphia Youth Center allows two or three service men to call their homes—or sweethearts!—during the rally, telephoning directly from the platform.

The unifying factor of the entire movement, however, is the pull for souls. Every one of these groups is out for the salvation of the thousands who are tagged with the dreadful word, "delinquency." It is the passion for souls that is uniting American youth today. One doubts that there ever will be a highly complex, nationally organized "Youth for Christ." Who knows? One thing we do know, however, when we look at what the Holy Spirit is doing in scores of cities today, that Christian young people are already united in a fresh realization that "now is the accepted time; behold, now is the day of salvation!"

CHAPTER SIX

GETTING STARTED IN YOUR TOWN

THE first, second, and third things to do in getting started are, in order of their importance:

1. Pray.   2. Pray.   3. Pray.

Organization is not the prime factor, as you might suppose. It *is* important, but more well-intentioned schemes have gone adrift upon the rocks of organizational prayerlessness than anywhere else!

We found it so in Chicago. Actually, our progress could have been charted in exact ratio to the intensity of our prayers. We moved well for a time, and all the machinery seemed to be functioning smoothly, when some unforeseen difficulty would show up, threatening the very life of the venture. Then, down on our knees we went, a little band of men who had asked God to keep their work on a miracle basis, and who were being reminded that miracles are God's methods—but that they depend on prayer!

There was prayer in Columbus the night of April 13, 1944, when "Chicagoland Youth for Christ" was born. There was earnest prayer in Chicago later on, when the first meeting of the staff was held. There was beseeching prayer when we were faced with the prospect of having a meeting—and no place to hold it. There was desperate prayer when radio channels all seemed to be blocked. And in all the turnings of everyday corners, prayer seemed to be the only way to get things done. God's expediters were forced to God's expedients—and how glad we are now that it was so!

Granted, then, that God has given you a vision for the work, and that you are definitely committed to a policy of prayer and faith, start working and praying for a staff adequate for the task.

It is a mistake to try to sell the idea to the community until you have something to sell. Organizations and individuals will co-operate more readily if they can see behind your plans and promotion some solid thinking and the presence of a competent staff to head up the work.

You need, for instance, good music. The old cliché, "special music," no longer holds an appeal for today's young people. They still thrill to good gospel melodies and messages, but they want the best.

Oddly, radio has spoiled things for the careless gospel musician; for your young folk can hear, if they wish, worldly music, *perfectly produced,* any hour of the day or night. It is not that they appreciate the gospel less, but that they have found out what good production is, and, brother, they'll hold you to it. Dare to offer them something shoddy, and they'll shun your meeting.

So, look for God's choice of musicians for your program. You need a pianist (or organist) with enough background to accompany well, and enough imagination to improvise upon familiar gospel themes. Nobody temperamental, please! You need a competent song leader who knows God. Bad song leading, or even good song leading with the flesh in it, can kill your meeting. For all your soloists and musical groups, emphasize high quality and spiritual sincerity. And always—rehearse, rehearse, rehearse! If someone wants to put on his number without rehearsal, tell him to take it elsewhere—you don't want it. Set this standard at the very start, and it will save you untold embarrassment later.

You'll need some one who knows publicity. Many good ideas die for lack of proper promotion. "Chicagoland Youth for Christ" was launched at the beginning of summer—what most Christians call the slack season—and in the face of such odds as that, good publicity helped a lot.

Now, find a place where the meeting can be held. It

ought to be a neutral spot, one that will appeal alike to saints and sinners, with equal attraction for members of various denominations. Some "Youth for Christ" movements are housed in large church auditoriums. This is good, but many feel that a large secular hall (like Kiel Hall, Orchestra Hall, or a Civic Auditorium, for instance) is better. Suit yourself, and ask God for His direct guidance in the matter. If God laid the work on your heart, He will tell you where to hold the meeting.

This word about size: Humanly speaking, you should select an auditorium that is just a little smaller than the crowd you anticipate. The world would class this as smart showmanship. Spiritually speaking, you ought to pray thoroughly enough to secure God's guidance, for He alone knows the size of the crowd He will send you. What if "Chicagoland Youth for Christ" had been launched in an auditorium seating only five hundred?

Some one asks: "What about radio? Must we have a broadcast?" The answer to that one would be this: In a youth program, dare we neglect the one thing which (with the possible exception of aviation) more nearly typifies the spirit of young people than anything else? Can you visualize the millions of G. I. Joes and G. I. Janes without including a mental image of their use of radio—both on and off the field of battle? Isn't radio a part of every youngster's environment today? Furthermore, doesn't the world present its best via radio? Then how can you conceive of a Christian youth program that does not include some broadcast in which the young people themselves can take part?

Now you begin to understand the persistence with which we prayed and worked to secure a broadcast for that first Saturday at Orchestra Hall. The radio period helps the people who listen to it—undoubtedly—but it helps the youngsters in the meeting even more, for they feel they are part of something big, and alive, and vital—and so they are!

If you can't get a "live" broadcast (direct from the place

of meeting), make a transcription. If you can't air the transcription that same night, take what time you can get, and pray for a better one. And if you can't get radio time at all, pray and work harder, and . . . God bless you!

Over the long pull, a "Youth for Christ" movement cannot be a one-man or one-church set-up. It must be co-operative and interdenominational, or fail of a truly great and representative ministry. Temporarily, any good promoter can "sell" himself and his program to a large following. But—we repeat it—over the *long* pull, he is dependent upon pastors, churches, city-wide youth organizations, and Christian leaders from all groups.

We faced that problem frankly and prayerfully. After we had sought the Lord's will in the matter, the answer seemed to be, "Ask, and ye shall receive." Ask we did, at two supper meetings in a down-town restaurant. The vision that God had given the founders was shared with groups of business people, and youth leaders. The present set-up was laid before them—Orchestra Hall, radio broadcast, a Spirit-sent personnel, a great heart burden for the lost. Then the blunt question: "What do you think of it? Do you want to help?" In every case, the answer was "Yes."

By "co-operation" we mean active help. Names on a letter-head in connection with the movement are all well and good—and we have them—but it was clearly understood from the beginning that those who were "in" were all the way in—to work! Accordingly, we put them on various jobs that ranged from distribution to personal work, from ushering to the provision of musical numbers from city-wide groups. Of course, everyone was supplied with "ammunition"—promotional literature of all kinds—and it must be said here to their credit that the people whose names appear on our advisory council and committee of recommendation have done a wonderful job. From the very start, and on through preparations for the Victory Rally at Chicago Stadium, we have received the finest kind of co-operation and practical help—this, from upwards of eighty people representing nearly a score of different denominations and twenty-five city-wide groups.

Co-operation involves problems immediately. We listed as many as we could think of, and faced them frankly. "Why not come out in the open with a declaration about some of these matters, instead of trying to dodge them?" we said. The result of this observation was our "Code for Success," a little document that was circulated in the audience during our first rallies, later printed and pasted in the back of our song books.

We faced the question of late hours, and said, "Get home before midnight—earlier teens by eleven."

We considered what a big Saturday night meeting might do to a Sunday school and church.

We realized the danger of criticism concerning proselyting, and we admonished, "Be loyal to your pastor, your church, and your city-wide young people's organization."

We know the tendency of all flesh to avoid work, so we urged, "There is work here for hundreds of consecrated young people. Find a place, and fill it."

Publicity and promotion was a big job in itself. Here is the way things shaped up in those early days:

1. City-wide distribution of hand cards, mailing cards, and posters. We circularized the pastors and churches, and loaded each of our committee members with "ammunition."

2. Adequate newspaper advertising, with pre-rally announcements three weeks before we started. News stories to fit each occasion were given to city and religious editors.

3. Ads in the leading evening newspapers of Chicago, with emphasis on a "different" kind of ad that would both attract attention and say something worth while.

4. Just before each rally, volunteer workers ranged through the Loop of Chicago, armed with tickets,

"Admit Two—Free" and tracts (donated 10,000 a week by one tract house) inviting strangers into the rallies. This procedure has paid out in the salvation of souls in several instances.

After a few weeks, we followed through with a couple of descriptive folders, and another poster, which advertised not only Orchestra Hall, but "plugged" our Victory Rally as well.

For the Victory Rally, through the excellent help of members of the committee, free advertising space on elevated platforms was secured, besides the regular routine of news stories, ads, and printed "pluggers."

It will pay you to spend money on good advertising. Remember, Jesus said, "The children of this world are in their generation wiser than the children of light" (Luke 16:8). Watch the clever advertisers in the world; they don't throw money away, but they are willing to invest heavily in something that will *pay*.

Here, then, is the set-up:

Pray

Get a staff

Find a place

Schedule a broadcast

Secure co-operation from pastors, laymen, city-wide youth groups.

Put people to work

Face problems frankly and fairly

Do a good job of advertising

Incidentally, here are some "don'ts" for those who contemplate trying a "Youth for Christ" in your community:

1. Don't alienate pastors and churches. You need them and they need you. Cultivate their confidence and support. Over the long pull, you succeed or fail in exact proportion as you have the good will of pastors and churches.

2. Don't make a typical adult gospel meeting out of it. Remember that this is YOUTH for Christ, and plan your program with teen age young people in mind.

3. Don't use the language of theology, nor the language of the street, but typical, wholesome, youth expressions. You are not addressing men and women, you're speaking to fellows and girls.

4. Don't let your program lag. Have well-planned variety, directed to a definitely evangelistic and missionary goal.

5. Don't build a Saturday night church. Plan to reach as many *new* people from week to week as possible. Remember, "Youth for Christ" means you have failed until you reach ALL the youth of your community for Him.

6. Don't ever try to put over an unprepared program. Young people can get what the world has to offer—perfectly prepared. If you have less, they'll leave you in a hurry.

7. Don't let your offerings degenerate to the level of a funny story and a specious plea for money. Keep your offerings on a high spiritual level, and God will bless you with sufficient funds.

8. Don't drag out your invitations. Young people are quick to resent the "tear-jerker" appeal, the "be-a-man" kind of challenge, the blunderbuss offer that gets anyone and everyone to the front. They want a straight-forward, hard-hitting gospel invitation—honest and fair.

9. Don't neglect to tell *all* your personnel exactly what is expected of them. Ushers should know where their place is, and what the planned procedure will be; personal workers should be coached in the matter of their approach to seekers, their routine in dealing with souls. Every person who has any part in the program should have a mimeographed copy of the program, timed to the second, so there will be no possible chance for mis-cues.

10. Don't be lax in your timing: start and stop your meeting on time.

A word about speakers: Get the very best available, even

if it involves bringing them from some distance. Make use of what you have in town, visiting evangelists, and such, ONLY if they qualify as young people's speakers. Many a good brother who can give out the Word to people in his certain bracket may go flat in a youth meeting.

Be sure your speaker understands what you are after. His twenty-two minutes are not to be spent in joking around and telling anecdotes, but in a straight-from-the-shoulder gospel message that has some "hooks" in it. Tell him to start preaching as soon as he has been introduced, and to fill every minute with the Word of God, given in power.

Unless you broadcast your entire rally, you may want to follow the two-message technique. This procedure involves a five to seven minute message on the air, and a longer (22-25 min.) message off the air, to wind up the meeting. Ordinarily we do not ask the visiting preacher to speak on the air, because the average person finds it impossible to say anything connected in such a short time—he generally compromises on a greeting and testimony. We must have a genuine gospel message on the air, therefore we have standardized on one speaker for the broadcast (Torrey Johnson almost always handles this work) and the visiting speaker for the closing message.

Much the same comment applies to the invitation. Not everyone knows how to give a gospel invitation—be sure you do before you try! If the leader of your "Youth for Christ" has had outstanding success in giving a gospel appeal, then it would probably be better to let him take the invitation after the main message. A smooth transition from speaker to leader can easily be effected, in prayer, or by some other device.

None of these directions is "sure-fire." You will have to work out your own routine, through prayer and thought and counsel together. Neither the means or methods used in Chicago, St. Louis, or New York, can be absolutely guaranteed to work, say, in Fresno or in Tallahassee. You might not want a meeting *every* Saturday night—alternate weeks might be better. Your budget might be more modest, or more lavish, depending on your local needs.

In any case, this movement is of the Holy Spirit. Take every problem to Him, and secure His infallible guidance. There is no failing, no missing the mark, with God.

CHAPTER SEVEN

RADIO—"THE LENGTHENED REACH"

FROM Orchestra Hall . . . CHICAGOLAND YOUTH FOR CHRIST!"

This "punchy" announcement by Torrey Johnson introduces the half-hour broadcast from Orchestra Hall every Saturday night. During the seconds before we go on the air, the pitch has been given from the organ, the audience has been rehearsed in their part, and now, the moment Johnson has given his announcement, the audience—three thousand strong—joins in singing,

"Christ lifted me, Christ lifted me!
When no one else could help, Christ lifted me."

The familiar theme with the words of "Love Lifted Me" continues through a verse and two choruses, and the broadcast is on its way. Beverly Shea, announcer and soloist extraordinary, gives the "commercial" while the audience is singing our sign-on theme.

The "flavor" of "Chicagoland Youth for Christ" broadcast comes not only from the personality of Master-of-Ceremonies Torrey Johnson, but also from the timing and pacing of the entire period. For instance, no time lag is allowed between numbers. The moment one is finished the next one is announced with very little unnecessary wordage. Emphasis is laid on *more* numbers with *fewer* stanzas, rather than more stanzas and fewer numbers.

Every announcement is "punchy" and has to do with the *significance* of the item to which it applies, as well as the *title*. This puts meaning and force in all that is said.

Highlight of the first part of the broadcast is the section given over to testimonies, where two or three outstanding young Christians are invited to give their personal witness for Christ. These testimonies are limited to forty-five seconds, and must be written out beforehand. This is a wise expedient because of the fact that in forty-five seconds, *ad lib,* the average person gets precisely nowhere. Testimonies written out in full insure accuracy and a minimum of stumbling.

Care is exercised to make these testimonies outstanding in every way. For instance, the testimony of a service man must come from one who has seen some special service or experience; the testimony of a medical man must represent noteworthy medical achievement; and the testimony of some person in ordinary life must represent one whose work as a layman has been characterized by unusual achievement for the Lord Jesus Christ. This precaution takes the testimonies out of the realm of mere talky-talk and insures listener interest.

Another musical number or two follows, then a five to seven-minute message by Director Torrey Johnson. His messages very frequently use some event of the day as a springboard. One of the most successful radio talks that Johnson ever gave, many think, was his message based on the "Red Cross." It starts by citing the experience that eight German Red Cross nurses had when, after their capture by the Allies, they were carted back across No Man's Land in an ambulance and returned to the German lines. Meanwhile, all shell fire ceased and the entire progress of the war waited upon the delivery of these Red Cross nurses safely back to their base. The similarity between the Red Cross and the Cross of the Lord Jesus Christ was graphically and forcefully presented that night. Other messages follow different leads, but every one of them has a true-to-life approach and a tremendous gospel appeal. Very frequently the gospel invitation is extended after one of these radio messages.

Sign-off chorus is the tender refrain of "I Surrender All." Many have said that it leaves the listener with the sustained impression of the pleading of the Holy Spirit.

If there is any secret of success in the radio portion of

"Chicagoland Youth for Christ," it is that every split second of the time is made significant in the light of a ministry to souls. Songs are "blood-gospel" songs, testimonies are strictly salvation testimonies, the message is a salvation message, everything is keyed to a salvation standard, and the appeal is straight-forward and direct.

This word about "commercials": They ought to be written so that the reader of the announcement will find no hissing sibilants or awkward phrasing, and they ought to be commercial in the best sense of the word; that is, that they help to "sell" the broadcast and the ministry to the radio audience.

The following radio messages by Torrey Johnson demonstrate the kind of impact your unseen audience must receive: brief, simple, direct, and always, crystal-clear gospel.

PROBLEMS NOT SOLVED BY SCIENCE
JUNE 3, 1944

One hundred years ago Samuel Morse sent the first message by telegraph. We celebrated the anniversary a few days ago. This was the first message—"WHAT HATH GOD WROUGHT."

I wish it were possible tonight to bring Samuel Morse to Chicago and have him with us on the platform of Orchestra Hall. I would like to have him look at the amplification system we have for this auditorium. I would like to have him speak into this microphone that carries my voice across the hundreds of miles and into the thousands of homes where people are listening tonight.

I wish he might hear the ring of a telephone, pick up the receiver, and hear a message from someone aboard ship at sea, someone in a plane in the air, someone in a submarine under the sea, someone from some other part of the world. I would like him to step down a few doors into the lobby of a hotel and put ten cents into a box. He would see before him marvelous things on the screen. While he looked, and listened and took in all of those things, I would like to ask, "Samuel Morse, what do you think about all that has been wrought in these one hundred years since that day you first sent that message across a few miles of these United States?"

Having presented to him that picture, I would take him across the avenues of Chicago to the courts of our city, to the courts of our county, and even to the Federal Court that is here in Chicago. As he stands there in those court rooms, I would have him listen to the description of the crimes that are being committed every day by teen age young people. I would take him into a divorce court and explain to him how during the month of May there were three divorces for every seven marriages here in the City of Chicago—three out of every seven marriages at the present time going on the rocks! I would take him into the Federal Court, and I would have him listen to the record of crimes and offenses that are being committed against the finest government in all the world.

Having first seen all the marvel of this mechanical age and then having gone into the court room to hear the categories of crime that have been committed, I would ask, "Samuel Morse, what do you think about all of this?" He would come to the same conclusions that every thinking man in our day comes to, and it is this:

While we are living in the most marvelous mechanical age, such as this world never before has known, at the same time we are living in the midst of sin, of trespasses, and of offenses of every kind, never before catalogued in all the ages of human history.

There are still three problems today that are not solved by science. The first is the problem of SIN, the second is the problem of the SOUL, and the third is the problem of ETERNAL DESTINY.

I am glad that I can say that the problem of sin was settled nineteen hundred years ago when Jesus Christ died for sin upon the Cross of Calvary. With outstretched hands, He says tonight, "Him that cometh unto me, I will in no wise cast out." "I am the way, the truth, and the life: no man cometh unto the Father but by me."

The second problem is the problem of the soul. I testify to you that all the research and all the good things that science has brought to us can never satisfy the soul of man. But Jesus Christ *can* satisfy the soul, as you heard from the testimonies of these three young friends a few moments ago.

Then I think of the problems that come to us day by day. I am glad that Jesus not only saves, He not only satisfies, but He also solves all the problems that we meet along life's way.

A young woman several weeks ago gave her heart to Jesus Christ. She took her engagement ring from her finger and laid it on the altar of the church and said within her heart, "I cannot marry that man. He is not a Christian. I will not marry him until he puts his trust in Jesus Christ." She wrote him a letter that she had accepted Jesus Christ and also told of her decision about their engagement. He came to the city of Chicago to see what was wrong. He saw her on Saturday. They were up late into the night. The following morning he continued again and throughout the day—he was going to straighten that girl out—but it was to no avail. She had found that Jesus Christ, when she placed her trust in Him, settled the question of sin in her life. She had found that Jesus Christ satisfied her soul as nothing else in all the world. She had found that Jesus Christ could solve all the problems that she met on life's way.

Toward the evening of Sunday, the young man was giving up, more or less, being discouraged and disgusted. The young woman said to him, "Come to the church where I was, listen to the man to whom I listened, and see if he has not something for you." They went into a certain church and there heard a young man preach. At the close of the message that night, her friend lifted his hand and said, "I want to take Jesus Christ into my heart and into my life. If Jesus Christ can take away the sin out of a life of the girl who has been my companion, if Jesus Christ can satisfy the longings of her soul, and if she has found in Him a friend that never fails, I too want Jesus Christ."

Several weeks went by, and there came a letter to the pastor of that church. In the letter was a sum of money, and also a notice that the man and this young woman had been united in marriage as a Christian young man and as a Christian young woman, establishing a Christian home. They also wrote, "We are sending this gift along, and we want you to know that this thing worked for one, and now it has worked for the other. We believe it is going to be good for our home in the days that lie ahead."

I wonder, my friend, in the midst of all the scientific inventions and all of these conveniences that we have today, whether you have settled the sin question. I wonder whether your soul is satisfied. I wonder about all your problems of life. Let me say to you tonight that Jesus Christ is adequate to meet every need for time and for eternity. While this company of friends blend their voices in singing, will you not trust yourself to Jesus Christ and accept Him as your personal Saviour from sin?

"D" DAY—DAY OF DESTINY

JUNE 10, 1944

It was midnight between June 5th and June 6th. The minute hand on Big Ben was making its way around to the midnight hour. That great clock, overlooking the Thames River in London, sounded out one, two, three, four, five, six, seven, eight, nine, ten, eleven and finally the midnight hour.

Out to the south of England, in the stealth of the darkness, there were 4,000 ships moving out to sea. They crossed about one hundred miles at the longest point of the English Channel, wending their way upon the greatest invasion that the world has ever known. Overhead, as these 4,000 ships pushed their way into the channel and across the sea, there were 11,000 planes, like an umbrella. The human eye can see in the skies overhead at one time about 1,000 planes. Here were 11 times more planes in the air than any man could see at one time. The planes dropped their cargo—paratroopers—inland on the invasion coast. The barges moved upon the beachheads, and out from the barges jumped large groups of young American, British, and Canadian soldiers, together with some French, and others of the Allies. They were moving in on one of the greatest battles, one of the most important events in all history.

As light dawned on June 6, the word was flashed around the world that it was "D" Day. It was the day of destiny. It was the day when the destiny of our Western civilization was hanging in the balance. It was the day of defeat for our enemies of many months' standing. It was the day of deliverance for those who had been captive in the hands of the oppressors in all the lands of Europe.

It was the day of devotion for young Americans, young British, young Canadians, and others of our Allies. What a day that was! We are still thinking now of that day. We are still praying now for those same young men and for that same cause.

As I think of "D" Day, the day of destiny, I think of another "D" day, another day of destiny—when an only Son slipped out of the portals of His Father's house and into the darkness of night. Far off from His Father's home into a little place that is called the world. In that world, the only begotten Son was born of a virgin in a manger in the little town of Bethlehem. After thirty years, having been reared in the town of Nazareth, He began his public ministry. He ministered for three years, teaching, preaching, and performing all kinds of miracles, even to the raising of the dead. When He was thirty-three years of age, they took Him one morning, as the light of a new day was breaking, from the garden where

He had been praying, to court for trial. From that court to another court, and then out beyond the gates of what they then called the Holy City, to be crucified upon a tree. That was a "D" Day that far exceeds what took place a few days ago. That was a day of destiny, the greatest of all days of destiny, because on that day Jesus Christ, the only begotten Son of God, died on the Cross of Calvary.

He brought defeat, not only to a temporal enemy, but He brought defeat to the eternal enemy of my soul. He brought defeat to Satan himself. When Jesus died upon the Cross of Calvary and cried, "IT IS FINISHED," He brought deliverance for every last man of Adam's race that was under the oppression of sin, that was shackled by the habits of evil, and under the dominion of the enemy of his soul. From that day to this, throughout nineteen hundred years, young men and young women, older men and older women have been devoted to the cause of Jesus Christ and have gone forth to the ends of the earth to testify to the saving grace, keeping power, and the satisfying power of this same blessed Lord and Saviour, Jesus Christ.

June 6th was the day of destiny for our Western civilization, but back yonder nineteen hundred years ago on a certain day, that has since become known as Good Friday, there was a day of destiny for all the human family. On that day Jesus Christ, God's Son, defeated Satan, brought deliverance for the human family. Around that same Saviour multitudes have followed in devotion, who have tasted to see that the Lord is good.

I am not interested today primarily in Good Friday. I am not interested alone in June 6. I am interested in this tenth day of June 1944, because this day can be the day of decision for many young men and young women. This can be a day when you decide to put your trust in Jesus Christ as your personal Saviour from sin. Scripture says, "As many as received him, to them gave he power to become the sons of God." "The wages of sin is death; but the gift of God is eternal life through Jesus Christ our Lord."

The day of destiny—June 6, 1944. It was a greater day of destiny when Jesus Christ died upon the Cross of Calvary. But may the day of decision, I pray, be today when you, just as you are, will thrown open your heart's door and let Jesus Christ come in and save your precious soul from sin. Do it now, out yonder as you listen and here in this auditorioum. Let Jesus come into your heart.

THINGS YOU CAN COUNT ON

JUNE 17, 1944

It was "D" Day. The word had gone around among the troops of the Allies that the hour had arrived for the invasion of Europe. Out from one of the secret hangars built into the side of a hill in the south of England, a crew wheeled their plane, ready to take off. Someone gave the order, and a group of about twenty paratroopers filed silently into that plane. They were huddled together in a group as the plane crossed those few miles across the channel to the Normandy coast of France. They looked at one another. They looked at their officers. Finally the word came. A door opened and in less time than it takes for me to tell you, those young men filed out into the darkness of that sky, one after another until all were gone. One of them descended into an open place, another near the bank of a stream, another in the edge of the woods, and so on—twenty different places.

Shortly after they had descended, they found their way to one another and then to the place that was their spot to hold while the troops came across in barges and otherwise, to invade the camp of the enemy and bring deliverance to those that were in bondage and in tyranny.

Every one of the paratroopers, every one of those fellows that rushed out from the barges, and the young women that were there to assist the wounded, were counting on certain things in those early days of that invasion.

They are still counting on certain things today. One of the things those young men were counting upon was the supply of every need that might arise in the course of the conflict. Another thing that they were counting upon was the co-operation of their officers, and the co-operation of all their buddies, that they might be one unit in facing a common foe. They also were counting upon directions, for one of the things that every one of those soldiers had was a map of the lands and terrain of Normandy, every creek, every road, every bridge, and every gun emplacement, as far as they knew it.

They were also counting upon enemy action. They knew it was not a Sunday school picnic to which they were going. They knew they were going to face the most terrific fire that the enemy could put together in one place at one time. But all those fellows were counting also on the fact that, at the close of those days of invasion, there would come a glorious victory. The people of the continent of Europe, who had been held in bondage, in suppression, and in tyranny, would once again be liberated.

I am telling you all of that this evening hour for this reason: When a young person receives the Lord Jesus Christ as his personal Saviour from sin, and he steps out into life with his new found friend and Saviour, there are certain things he too may count upon.

That young person who receives Christ as his personal Saviour may count upon the supply of every need through faith in Jesus Christ. Paul the Apostle said, "My God shall supply all your need according to his riches in glory by Christ Jesus." Young fellow in uniform in this company tonight, let me tell you without reservation, you will find that Jesus Christ never fails the young man. He never fails the young woman who puts her trust in Him as Saviour and embraces Him as Lord.

Again, just as those who invaded the coast of Normandy were counting upon the co-operation of their officers and buddies, so you can count on the co-operation of the Captain of your Salvation. Paul said, "I can do all things through Christ which strengtheneth me." We sometimes hear in a humorous vein of officers being in the rear lines. I am glad that in this conflict in which we are now engaged, the generals of the United States Army and the leading officers have been out in the front with the men. I tell you tonight that Jesus Christ goes out into the front WITH every man and FOR every man that puts his trust in Jesus Christ as his personal Saviour. You can count on the Captain of your Salvation.

Furthermore, just as those fellows had a map that outlined for them all of the land, so you can find direction for your life in the blessed Holy Spirit who comes to take His abode in your heart. The moment you receive Christ as your Saviour, you will hear a voice behind you saying, "This is the way, walk ye in it."

Just as every one of those young men were counting upon the enemy action, so you can count upon every kind of evil force to work in opposition to you when you put your trust in Jesus Christ as your Saviour. But let me say this: "Greater is he that is in you, than he that is in the world."

Just as the boys out there on the invasion coast are counting on victory, so we have the assurance of victory over sin, over the grave, and over the enemy of our souls, through faith in Jesus Christ our blessed Saviour.

Have you trusted in Christ? One young man said that it was harder for him to open his heart to Jesus Christ than it was for him to crawl across those front lines in the face of enemy gun fire. I know that the hardest thing any man or woman, young fellow or girl ever did was to throw open the heart and let Jesus come in. Young fellow, I challenge you to let Jesus come in as your Saviour. Young woman, I challenge you to throw open the the door of your heart and let Jesus Christ demonstrate just what He can mean in your life.

THE CHRISTIAN: HIS PLATFORM
AND CANDIDATE

JUNE 24, 1944

Chicago this year once again welcomes two great national conventions, the convention of the Republican party which opens on Monday evening of next week, and then in the month of July, Chicago welcomes the Democratic party. They will convene in our great city to select their candidates to run for president, and for vice president. They will establish a platform on which they are to operate and prosecute the plans for which they hope to be successful in the November elections.

I have been thinking during these days about the platform. I have been thinking also about the party candidates. My mind has been thinking again of the plan of campaign.

I am so glad I am a Christian tonight and that the Christian has a platform that is absolutely incomparable. These conventions and these men, as they gather from the forty-eight states of the Union and the various territories, are to develop, submit, and adopt a platform for the four years to come. The platform that I find in this Book which I hold in my hand, God's Holy Word, is a platform not only for time but for all eternity. The platform that these men are to adopt for four years to follow has to do with the temporal and material needs of men. The platform that I find in this Book has to do with the eternal and spiritual needs of men. As I compare the two platforms, each with the other, I find in the Bible so much more than the very best that the political parties of our country or of the world could possibly offer. These platforms deal with the needs and problems of your life. This Book deals with the needs and problems not only for this life, but also for the life that is to come.

I think not only of the platform, but I think also of

the party candidates. I do not know tonight whom the Republicans will select. I am quite confident I know whom the Democrats will select. But be that as it may, no matter whom these men may select to run for president of the United States in the November election, these things are true of both of those men: First, that whoever it may be who runs for president, he is a man of imperfect character. No matter how good a man he may be— "All have sinned, and come short of the glory of God." "There is no difference." Paul said, "I know that in me (that is, in my flesh,) dwelleth no good thing." The second thing about these candidates who will be elected next week end and in the month of July is that they are imperfect in their knowledge. They do not know it all. In fact they know very little about what is going to transpire in the next four years. They know very little what may transpire in the next twelve months. The third thing about these candidates is that they are imperfect in their ability to fulfill the promises that their party may make. They are imperfect in character. They are imperfect in knowledge. They are imperfect in ability.

Now I turn from these candidates who are to run for the high office of president of the United States, and I read of that Man concerning whom all of the twenty-seven books of the New Testament speak and the thirty-nine books of the Old Testament foretell. I find One who is perfect in His character, perfect in His knowledge and perfect in His ability.

I am so glad for that because there are four things that I am especially concerned about. I am concerned about the answer to life's greatest question, and the White House does not have the answer to life's greatest question. Life's greatest question is sin, and Jesus Christ, God's only Son, has the answer to the sin question. "He who knew no sin was made to be sin for us that we might be made the righteousness of God in Him." Jesus Christ is my candidate for time and for eternity. Our lieutenant friend of the U. S. Marines said a few moments ago that he salutes Jesus Christ. I say with him that I also salute Him, not only salute Him but embrace Him as my Saviour and as my Lord. He is the One in whom I have confidence both for this life and for that which lies beyond.

Again, Jesus Christ has the answer to life's greatest fear—death. No young man in the Army, Navy, or Marines; no young woman in any of the branches of the Service need have any fear of any kind if he or she has Christ in his heart. Jesus Christ takes the fear of death *out* of their hearts and brings the assurance of life eternal to their soul.

Jesus Christ has the answer to life's greatest quest— the quest for life itself. Jesus Christ said, "I am come that they might have life, and that they might have it more abundantly." Jesus Christ is my candidate tonight. God's Word is my platform tonight, and I am voting a straight ticket in that direction.

Again, Jesus Christ has the answer to life's greatest question, "Where are we going from here?" He said, "I go to prepare a place for you. And if I go and prepare a place for you, I will come again, and receive you unto myself; that where I am, there ye may be also."

I do not know tonight whether you are a Republican or a Democrat. I am not so concerned about those things. But I am vitally concerned about your attitude toward you and your personal relationship to Jesus Christ, God's candidate, the one whom God presents as the Saviour from sin, the one who can give you life eternal, if you will trust in Him as your all.

If you have never embraced the Lord Jesus Christ as your Saviour, as you listen to my voice here in the auditorium, and in your homes, will you not throw open the door of your heart and say, "Yes, I have been interested in the political candidate. I have been interested in things of this life, but the things that are eternal are of vital consequence. I will put my trust in Jesus Christ as my personal Saviour."

THE RED CROSS AND THE CROSS OF CHRIST

JULY 8, 1944

In Galatians 6:14 we read—"But God forbid that I should glory, save in the cross of our Lord Jesus Christ, by whom the world is crucified unto me and I unto the world."

This afternoon there stepped into my study a young woman with her fiance. He was a sergeant in the United States Army. They said, "Let's get it over with in a hurry." The young man looked at me and said, "This uniform is awfully hot. Make it as short as you can." I did exactly what they wanted me to do, but, nevertheless, I packed in a lot of the truth of God's word. Immediately after the ceremony we were talking a little bit about his going back to Camp Shelby, Miss., and their future in these days of the war. Among other things that we talked about was the allotment that would come to his new bride. I said, "I do not know much about allotments. I always turned over all of my check to my wife. I am sure of this, however, that if you go to the Red Cross, they can help you out."

You know the Red Cross is a marvelous institution, not only here in America but among all the nations of the world, in Japan, Germany, and Italy as well as in France, England and the United States. The Red Cross is here to help. Not only does the Red Cross help those who are in difficulty, but I know that many of you have sent and received messages, through this great international organization, from people in other parts of the world.

In addition, there is protection in the Red Cross. Let a Red Cross be painted on the roof of a hospital, school, or some other institution, and by international law and the observation of the international law, that school or hospital is to be protected because of one thing and one thing only—the RED CROSS.

Again, the Red Cross guarantees safety in transit. There

are many people traveling the high seas or the oceans to-day in perfect safety because of the Red Cross flags, because of the Red Cross emblem painted on the roof of the deck and upon the sides of those ships.

This account was interesting to me as I read it in the paper a few days ago. Among those who were captured on the Normandy beachhead were eight Red Cross nurses associated in the German Army. A time was arranged when the firing of American and German guns would cease. An ambulance left the American lines with these eight German Red Cross nurses in it. At the same time from the German lines there left another automobile. They met in no man's land, between the two front lines. There in that place these eight Red Cross nurses were exchanged and moved from the ambulance of the Americans to the German automobile and were whisked back of the German lines in safety. After that the gun-fire began once more.

Now, why was it that when thousands of German prisoners were sent across the channel to prisoner camps in Britain and in America, these eight nurses were per-mitted to go free? Because they were members of the Red Cross.

I have told you these five tremendous truths about the Red Cross tonight for this reason: I find those things true not only in relationship to the Red Cross, but I find those things eternally and spiritually true in the Cross of our Lord and Saviour Jesus Christ. There is protection accord-ing to the will of God for those who put their faith and trust in Jesus Christ as their Saviour. It is by the blood of Jesus that we have access into the presence of God with all the messages, petitions, and the burdens of our hearts. There is help through the medium of the Cross of Christ, for we read, "Let us therefore come boldly unto the throne of grace, that we may . . . find place to help in time of need." There is safety from this world for those who have trusted in Jesus Christ. The man who has trusted in Christ is never any longer a prisoner to Satan or to sin for "if the

Son therefore shall make you free, ye shall be free indeed."

I have been a member of the Red Cross for many years, and I have received benefits from many sources. Among all the benefits I have ever received, the greatest of them all is salvation, full and free, through the Cross of my blessed Lord and Saviour Jesus Christ.

My friend, if you have never trusted in the Cross of Christ and in the Christ of the Cross, if you have never received Him as your personal Saviour from sin, I would encourage you and I would challenge you to throw open the door of your heart and let Jesus Christ come in and save your precious soul tonight. "God forbid that I should glory, save in the cross of our Lord Jesus Christ, by whom the world is crucified unto me, and I unto the world."

THE ONLY INDISPENSABLE MAN

JULY 22, 1944

In recent years we have been hearing a great deal about the "indispensable man." I propose to speak to you tonight about that man.

A few days ago a doctor recommended that I call on a certain man that had become enslaved to the evil habit of drink. The call was made, and after the call, he responded to the invitation to come to church. At the close of the evening service last Sunday night, that man came forward indicating he would receive Jesus Christ into his heart. He was dealt with afterwards; he was prayed with, and went on his way, we trust, with Christ in his heart and a new power in his life.

That man needed two things especially. The first thing he needed was a power that would liberate him from the enslavement of sin. The second thing he needed at that moment was a cleansing of his heart and life from the guilt of sin. That Sunday evening as he knelt with others and prayed, "God be merciful to me a sinner, and save me now for Jesus' sake," he found that this One who was absolutely indispensable to him did those two things for him. He found that by faith first of all Jesus Christ could cleanse his heart from sin. He found also that the same faith which led him to trust Christ, released for him a power that enabled him to have victory over all sin.

The man, the only man, the man who can truthfully say he is the "Indispensable Man" is Jesus Christ, and He said it in John 14:6—"Jesus saith unto him, I am the way, the truth, and the life: no man cometh unto the Father, but by me." Again in John 10:9 He said, "I am the door: by me if any man enter in, he shall be saved."

Peter found that Jesus Christ was indispensable in his life, for Peter said in Acts 4:12, "Neither is there salvation in any other: for there is none other name under heaven given among men, whereby we must be saved." The great Apostle Paul found that Jesus Christ was the Indispensable Man, for in I Timothy 2:5, Paul said, "For there is one God, and one mediator between God and men, the man Christ Jesus." And for nineteen hundred years men and women that have trusted in Jesus Christ as their personal Saviour from sin have testified to the fact that He is the one pre-eminently indispensable man for any man and any woman, and He is indispensable for these reasons:

First, because He alone can cleanse from the guilt of sin. Second, because He alone can liberate from the power of sin. Third, because He alone can fully satisfy, and fourth, because He alone can give me perfect assurance.

We have been hearing in recent days about the "abundant life." Jesus Christ first pronounced those words when He said, "I am come that they might have life, and that they might have it more abundantly." I tell you tonight that the more abundant life is found not in some political theory or philosophy of government, it is found in Jesus Christ. Here are multiplied hundreds that would stand out and testify to the fact that Jesus Christ was indispensable, because when they tried everything

— 61 —

and everyone else, they found that Jesus alone could satisfy.

Again, He is the Indispensable Man because He alone can open Heaven's doors. He didn't say, "I am *a* door." There isn't a Christian way, a Buddhist way, a Unitarian way, a Humanitarian way—there is only one way, and Jesus Christ is that Indispensable way, for He said, "I am *the* door."

I say to you tonight that it is not only a good thing, but it is an absolute necessity to put your trust in the Lord Jesus Christ if you are to be saved for time and for eternity. I know that in this vast audience there are hundreds and thousands who have never bowed the knee and by simple faith received Christ into your heart as your own personal Saviour from sin. You think you need this person or that person; there are voices clamoring for certain ones that are indispensable for a period of time, but . . . they may die one of these days! I'm so glad that the Scripture tells us "he is able also to save them to the uttermost that come unto God by him, seeing *he ever liveth* to make intercession for them."

I have found that Jesus is the indispensable man, and I've found that Jesus satisfied my soul. He liberated me from the enslavement of sin; He pardoned me from the guilt of my sin; He cleansed my heart; and He gave me the assurance that when I shove off from here, I'm going where the gates swing outward never, where there's a welcome for all who come.

If you have never yielded to Christ, may I encourage you to throw open the door of your heart and say, "Jesus, I've tried others, now I'm willing to take Thee as my personal Saviour from sin. . . . God's Indispensable Man."

CHAPTER EIGHT

MESSAGES GOD USED IN WINNING SOULS AT ORCHESTRA HALL

FROM the outset, it was plain that the meetings at Orchestra Hall demanded a certain type of message. It must be slanted for young people, to gain and hold inter; est; clear gospel and helpful Christian life truth must be packed into those brief 22 minutes; and, above all, the messages must lead naturally into a definite invitation to receive Christ.

The messages in this chapter are representative of the kind that "got results."

FOUR LOOKS AT CHRIST

Message delivered by Wendell P. Loveless, Director,
Radio Department, the Moody Bible Institute, Chicago,
June 10, 1944

Recently, while reading some excerpts from a very old book, I found the words of a distinguished theologian of another day. They were his expression of that which he conceived to be the message of the gospel of the grace of God.

The words are these:

> "Christ, absolutely necessary,
> Christ, instantly accessible,
> Christ, exclusively sufficient,
> Christ, perennially satisfying."

As one meditates upon those words, he feels that they

epitomize the very heart of the good news concerning eternal salvation in Christ.

The Scriptures tell us of at least four views of Christ which are possible to the eye of faith, which parallel these four statements by our old theologian concerning Him.

The true believer, through the eye of faith, sees the Lord Jesus

> On the cross,
> In the glory,
> Indwelling the Christian,
> Coming again.

First we look at Christ *on the cross*.

Here, the view reveals "Christ, absolutely necessary." Paul the Apostle, in Romans 3:10, declares, "There is none righteous, no, not one," and Romans 3:23, ". . . for there is no difference: for all have sinned, and come short of the glory of God."

God Himself has met the eternal need of sinful man. God has demanded perfect righteousness from man. Man cannot give God any righteousness acceptable unto Him. What is God's remedy? The Cross of our Lord Jesus Christ, the shed blood of God the Son.

Listen to the words of II Corinthians 5:21, "For he (God) hath made him (Christ) to be sin for us, who knew no sin; that *we might be made the righteousness of God in him.*"

God has required *of* man perfect righteousness. God has supplied *to* man perfect righteousness. That perfect righteousness is not merely an attitude; it is a Person— the person of our Lord Jesus Christ.

An old Puritan gave a definition of the righteousness of God which was something as follows: "The righteousness of God is that righteousness which the righteousness of God requires him to require." Such is the person of our blessed Lord.

Without this look at Christ on the cross, we can have no eternal life, no eternal salvation, no forgiveness of sins. But when we "look to the Lamb of God," we have, in

Him, all that we need for time and for eternity. "The wages of sin is death; but the gift of God is eternal life through Jesus Christ our Lord" (Rom. 6:23).

I wonder if things are as *personal* to us as they should be. Suppose you should come to me today and say, "I see by the papers that a man died today in Chicago." I probably would reply, "Yes, people are dying right along in every city all over the world." "But this man was a very wealthy man," you might say. "Yes," might be my rejoinder, "rich people die, just the same as poor people." "Oh, but this man left over a million dollars!" "Yes, if he left *anything*, I am sure he left it all," I would say, not exhibiting any great interest. "But, wait a minute," you might remark, "he left it all to *you*." "Oh, well, that's different!" Now there is genuine interest, because it has become *personal*.

Christ died for *all*, but he died for *each*. God loves *all*, but He loves *each*. Salvation is offered to *all*, but it is offered to *each*. *All* who *will* may be saved; *you* may be saved. God's offer of grace is to *all*; it is personal to *you*.

Christ on the cross; "*Christ, absolutely necessary.*" But, thank God, our blessed Lord did not remain on the cross, or in the tomb. The crucifix is not the true symbol of our faith.

And so the eye of faith, in the second place, looks at Christ, risen and *in the glory*. This view reveals "*Christ, instantly accessible.*"

Having seen the Lord Jesus, dying *for* us and *as* us on the cross, bearing "our sins in his own body on the tree" (I Pet. 2:24), we need to see Him risen again out from among the dead, exalted to His present position at the right hand of the Father.

Paul, writing to his son in the faith, Timothy, (II Tim. 2:8) exhorts him to "remember that Jesus Christ was raised from the dead." He is alive; He is the man in the Glory; He is not some disembodied spirit; but He is the Glorified Man.

We must remember that no statement of "the gospel

of the grace of God" is complete without the declaration of the resurrection of our Lord.

A man stood in an art gallery, before a striking picture of Christ on the cross. As he gazes upon that solemn and significant scene, he was conscious of a little form standing at his side. He turned and saw a ragged urchin, whom he asked, "Do you know who that is?" "Sure," replied the boy, "don't *you* know?" "Who is it?" asked the man. "Why, that's Jesus." "What's He doing there?" "They killed Him, and He died for our sins." "Where did you learn that, sonny?" "At the Mission Sunday school." The man moved along the gallery arcade, but had not gone far before he heard the patter of little feet, and felt a tug at his coat. He turned and saw his little friend of a moment before. "Hey, Mister." "Yes?" "He came alive again." The little fellow remembered that which we so often forget, that the gospel is not complete without the resurrection.

Christ is at the right hand of the Father, our *High Priest,* to pray for us—One who can "be touched with the feeling of our infirmities" (Heb. 4:15). He is there, and "ever liveth to make intercession for them" (Heb. 7:25). He is there to be our *Advocate,* when we sin (I John 2:1, 2). He is there our *representative* with the Father. He is the "Firstfruits" of a multitude who shall one day be with Him and like Him in the Glory.

Because He lives, we may come boldly unto the throne of grace, into the very presence of the Father, to make our requests known. We are accepted in Christ. The Father hears us and receives us because now He sees us in His beloved Son.

We need no earthly, human priest, to intercede for us, for every true believer, however humble, has immediate, welcome access, through Christ, into the very presence of God.

'Tis not for *works* which I have wrought,
'Tis not for *gifts* which I have brought,
Nor yet for *blessings* which I sought,
    That I have been "accepted."

'Tis not for *tears* which I have shed,
'Tis not for prayers that I have said,
Nor yet for slavish fear or dread,
    That I have been "accepted."

'Tis not for *truth* which I believed,
'Tis not for *grace* which I received,
Nor yet for *thankful words* I breathed,
    That I have been "accepted."

'Tis not for *sorrows* which have grown
From *evils* which were all mine own,
Nor yet for *pleading* at the Throne,
    That I have been "accepted."

From these I turn my eyes to Him
Who bore my judgment due to sin,
And by His blood I enter in,
    And share in His acceptance.

Christ in the Glory; Christ, instantly accessible.

In the third place, the eye of faith looks at Christ *dwelling within the believer*. This view reveals Christ, exclusively sufficient.

The words of Galatians 2:20 come to mind, "I am crucified with Christ; nevertheless I live! yet not I, but *Christ liveth in me*: and the life which I now live in the flesh I live by the faith of the Son of God, who loved me, and gave himself for me."

The risen, glorified Christ, in the person of the Holy Spirit, has taken up His abode, His abiding place, in the body of every true child of God. He used seven wonderful words in John 14:20, "Ye in me, and I in you."

I Corinthians 6:19, "Know ye not that your body is the temple of the Holy Ghost which is in you, which ye have of God, and ye are not you own?"

As God the Father came to earth in the Person of the Son, so Christ the Son dwells within us in the Person of the Holy Spirit. Christ lives within us to strengthen, enable, and use us: *He does not ask us to imitate Him,* but to *yield* ourselves to Him, and our members as instruments of righteousness unto Him. He will use us. He does not ask us to use Him.

A Christian leader used to express it thus: "Supposing

I woke up in the morning and found the blessed Lord standing by my bedside, and He would say to me, 'My child, were you satisfied with your life yesterday?'"

"No, Lord, I was not."

"Rather bad, wasn't it?"

"Yes, very bad, Lord."

"What were you trying to do yesterday, my child?"

"Well, Lord, I was trying to imitate you."

"Well, now, suppose we try another way. I can enter into you; suppose you just yield your members now to Me as instruments of righteousness. That is all I ask of you—yield your thoughts, your whole nature to Me. Yield your passions to Me; yield to Me your entire being. I will enter in and take possession, and we'll try it that way for a day. Stop trying. Stop fighting. Let Me do the trying—everything."

Everyone of us would gladly welcome the Lord thus, wouldn't we? Ah, but He *is* within us. And when the eye of faith sees Him thus, it means victory in every department of our lives.

Christ indwelling the believer; Christ, exclusively sufficient.

Finally, the eye of faith looks at *Christ coming again*. This view reveals *Christ, perennially satisfying*. This view of Christ is called, in Scripture, "that blessed hope" (Titus 2:13).

The Lord Jesus Christ is coming again, personally, visibly, just as He came the first time, personally and visibly. He is coming *for* His own people first, and then *with* His own to rule and reign over the earth.

One of these days, we shall hear the "shout . . . the voice of the archangel, and . . . the trump of God: and the dead in Christ shall rise first: Then we which are alive and remain shall be caught up together with them in the clouds, to meet the Lord in the air: and so shall we ever be with the Lord" (I Thess. 4:16, 17).

The Psalmist said, "As for me, I will behold thy face

in righteousness: I shall be satisfied, when I awake, with thy likeness" (Psalm 17:15).

Christ coming again; Christ, perennially satisfying.

The things of earth do not satisfy. They are exceedingly uncertain these days. But the Christian has a glorious and satisfying prospect. His future is as glorious and as sure as is the future of Christ!

> Lord Jesus, I have found in Thee
>   Abundant *life;*
> Life that as a river floweth,
> Life that deeper, fuller groweth
>   'Mid earth's strife.
>
> Lord Jesus, I have found in Thee
>   Eternal *peace;*
> Peace which passeth understanding,
> Peace which day by day expanding,
>   Shall not cease.
>
> Lord Jesus, I have found in Thee
>   Exceeding *joy;*
> In Thy presence joy forever,
> Joy which even Satan never
>   Can destroy.
>
> Lord Jesus, I have found in Thee
>   The *love* of God;
> Perfect love that never faileth,
> Love which evermore availeth
>   By Thy blood.

"YE MUST BE BORN AGAIN"

Message delivered by Dr. Archer Anderson,
Pastor, First Presbyterian Church, Duluth, Minn.,
Saturday, July 29, 1944

I would like to ask you some questions tonight and have you think about them. They are based on an experience recorded in the second and third chapters of the Gospel of John. Do you think it is possible for a young person actually to come to the place where he makes a profession of faith in Jesus Christ and still not be saved? I wonder whether it would be possible for someone to come into the presence of the Son of God, to hold His hand, to sit beside Him, to walk with Him, be in His school for three years and still not be saved? I wonder whether it would be possible for someone to preach in the name of Christ, yes, more than that, to be one of the group sent out to cast out demons—to have so much power that even the demons were subject to him in the name of Christ. Could a person be like that and still not be saved? My Bible tells me that he can! His name was Judas.

In the second chapter of John we read about a number of people who *said* that they were disciples of Jesus Christ. When our Lord was in Jerusalem at the Passover on the feast day, many believed in His name when they saw the miracles that Jesus did, but Jesus did not trust Himself to them. Why not? Didn't they *say* they believed in His name? Didn't they bear testimony to the fact that the miracles that Jesus was performing proved to them that He was the Messiah, the one that they looked for and expected and wanted to follow? Yes, just like a lot of folk today. You know, a lot of folk who talk about heaven aren't going there. But Jesus didn't trust these people. Why not? You read it yourself in the twenty-fourth and twenty-fifth verse: "But Jesus did not commit himself unto them, because he knew all men, And needed not that any should testify of man (here it is); for he knew what was in man." That's a tremendous statement.

In the early ministry of our Lord He turned the water into wine; He did other miracles and the great throngs rose up to follow Jesus, or so they said. Why? They wanted an easy life. They didn't want to be turned from sin but from work. This man could feed five thousand people—all they had to do was to sit down and eat the food as it was put before them. This man could heal anybody who was sick—they didn't have to worry about doctor's bills. This man could quiet the water—if there was a storm on the lake, they could go fishing and not be afraid. I would like to follow a man like that, wouldn't you? They didn't want salvation. They wanted a good time! They wanted a Saviour who could be cut down to their pattern. Just like an x-ray can see through your body, so the eyes of Jesus Christ can see through your heart as He saw through theirs. He didn't trust them—I wonder if He trusts you?

Is it possible to have your name on the rolls of the church and not be saved? Is it possible to be an officer in the church and not be saved? We had something that was like an earthquake in Duluth a couple of years ago in the Presbyterian Church. After a simple gospel message, I gave an invitation and to the utter consternation of all present, one of the elders came down the aisle to be saved.

Now that was not a modernistic church. It had its seventy-fifth birthday and never yet has it tolerated any man in the pulpit who doesn't preach the whole Word of God. I met with the elder in the inquiry room and said, "What are you doing here?"

I'll never forget his answer. He said, "Doc, you keep talking about being born again and I don't know what you're talking about."

He suddenly understood what had been the matter with him all the time, but it isn't the matter any more because he met Jesus Christ.

That brings us to this third chapter of John. I would like to have you get the picture because it is of tremendous importance. A lot of people saw His miracles and maybe some of them said, "Master, I'll follow you wherever you go . . . just so you'll feed me." That was in their hearts. But Jesus didn't trust them. He didn't reveal Himself to them because they weren't saved.

But there was one man, a man of the Pharisees, named Nicodemus. That man came to Jesus by night, just as you and I would do. He stepped over to where Christ was, greeted him with a very nice salutation, and paid Him high honors. I suppose he curtsied a wee bit and said, "Rabbi . . ." That was a tribute, for he was a graduate of many seminaries in Israel, and Jesus was just the adopted son of a carpenter. But this great religious leader said,

"Rabbi, we know that thou art a teacher come from God: for no man can do these miracles that thou doest, except God be with him."

The Lord Jesus turned and said, "Nicodemus, you just don't know me. You, Nicodemus, must be born again."

Let's jump across the centuries from Nicodemus. I wonder what would happen if you were to meet the Lord Jesus face to face as Nicodemus did? You would step up and say, "Good evening, Lord. I'm so happy I can meet you tonight. Lord, I have memorized 172 verses from the Bible, and I can say them all without any mistake. Yes, I can even give the references."

And Jesus would say, "You've got to be born again!"

Maybe you would meet Him and say, "Good evening, Lord. My dad is a deacon in the great Baptist Church."

He would look at you and say, "Is that so? You've got to be born again."

That reminds me of a young lady at our church in Duluth. She and her boy friend were at a young people's conference, and as I was making the rounds I noticed that there was somebody in a car so I walked around carefully. I didn't want to surprise them too suddenly, and the car door pushed open and out came Bill. He said, "I knew this was one way to get to see you. Audrey wants to talk to you. Good night, Doc. I'm leaving." And away he went.

I stood by the door looking at Audrey and said, "What's the matter with you anyway?" I noticed that she didn't seem to be very happy, and she said, "Doc, you know I think I'm going to Hell and I can't believe it."

"What do you mean, you can't believe it?" I asked.

"Why," she said, "my father is an elder in the First Presbyterian Church."

"Yes," I said, "and his daughter, just like her daddy, is nothing but a sinner that needs to be saved. Girl, you need to be born again"—and she was!

You must be born again—that's what Christ would say to you tonight, everyone of you. He would cut right through all the superficial profession of faith that you and I have made. He wouldn't be satisfied with words from your lips. He would look right straight into your heart, and He would find one of two things. He would either find Himself, or He would find sin. He would say, "Young person, you need to be born again." Nicodemus did the natural thing. He was non-plussed; you would be too. He had an experience that took him down.

Some years ago I went as a missionary to Guatemala. I was full of life and anxious to go to work and said, "I wish I could speak Spanish." One of the co-workers said, "Thank God, you can't."

"What do you mean?"

"You'd be like a bull in a china shop if you could. You better get alone and study," he said.

What a rebuke that was. It would be like that if you met Jesus tonight. You would come up like Nicodemus and say, "We know you are a divine teacher. They taught me that you are the Son of God. Lord, they even taught me that you died on the cross and rose again. I can repeat the Apostle's creed in its entirety."

The Lord would say, "Stop, you have to be born again."

Nicodemus said, "HOW can I be born again? Can I become a babe again?" I'll tell you something. It wouldn't do me any good if I could. I would still be "just me," and "just me" is not good enough to go to Heaven, and neither is "just you," because "That which is born of the flesh is flesh; and that which is born of the Spirit is spirit." You must be born *of God*. But you say, "Didn't God make me?" Sure He did, but that doesn't mean you're His child.

Before going to Guatemala I happened to use a verse of scripture in a sermon taken from the Lord Jesus Christ when He said, "Ye are of your father the devil." After the service a couple of men came to me with doubled fists and were going to take me apart. I couldn't understand what it was all about. I said, "Why are you so angry?"

They said, "You told us that we are the children of the devil."

I said, "No, I didn't."

"You did so."

Again I said, "I did not.'

They said, "You said it and we heard you, and we are not the children of the devil."

"I didn't say that," I said. "That was Jesus Christ who said it. If you want to fight, fight with Him, don't fight with me."

I can still see that one fellow as he said, "So you think we are children of the devil. Let me ask you something. Who made us? Did the devil or God?"

I said, "You don't look much like it, but God made you." They didn't particularly like that, but I thought they had it coming.

He looked up and said, "That proves it. You yourself said God made us. Then we are the children of God."

I pointed to a bench and said, "Who made that?" They looked surprised and said, "We don't know." I said, "Sure you do." One said, "I suppose the carpenter did." I said, "That's right. That makes the bench the daughter of the carpenter, doesn't it?" They thought there was something wrong with me and they said so. I said, "No, I just followed your reasoning. Why isn't the bench the daughter of the carpenter?" The answer was, "Because the bench doesn't have the life of the carpenter in it." So I said, "You are the creation of God, but you are not the sons of God for exactly the same reason the bench is not the daughter of the carpenter—you do not have the life of God until you are born again." But how can you be born again? By simply accepting the gospel as given in that great text, John 3:16, that Christ was to become the sacrifice for us, that He would perform the greatest miracle of all history, that God could take your sins from you and nail them on His Son and let His Son on Calvary bear your sins and satisfy God's holiness and open the way for you to be born again—that's the greatest miracle of all time.

Have you ever had anybody offer to die for you? I did when I was in Guatemala. I sent a telegram one day to another member of the mission, and purposely made it ambiguous. One of the missionaries had done something she shouldn't have, and it looked like she might have to go home. However, I didn't know that there was a revolution to come off on the very day I specified in the telegram, in a place called Santa Anna. When I sent the telegram, the three key words of the revolution, unknown to me, were in the telegram. The telegram went not to the missionary, but to the president, and he sent out orders immediately to arrest Archer Anderson. They have a very convenient way of holding a trial there. They take the prisoner and shoot him first. Then, if they find that he wasn't guilty, they apologize to his family.

I didn't know anything about this until some time later when a man named Santiago was talking to me as we sat in my car. He said, "I'm sorry, but I have to ask you a personal question. What did you mean by your telegram?" I asked, "What do you know about it?"

Then he told me the story. He said, "Your telegram went to the president, and he sent it to the General. The General instead of arresting you, sent for me. He said, 'Look, there is a revolution in Santa Anna on Monday. This man sends a telegram mentioning Santa Anna and Monday. What is the meaning of all this?'"

Santiago said, "I took my hat off, stood up, and said, 'General, I'm his hostage.'"

He said, "Santiago, don't be a fool. Don't you know what will happen?"

"I certainly do, but I'm his hostage." He was standing instead of Anderson in the place of judgment.

The general said, "But Santiago, it might cost your life."

"That's all right, I'm willing."

"Why should you be willing?" the general asked.

"Because he led one of my children to Christ."

The general said, "If you are willing to trust him that

much, I'll trust him too. But you find out what that telegram was about."

He looked at me and said, "What are you crying about?"

I said, "That's the first time I had anybody offer to die for me." It got down under my skin because nobody ever did that for me before.

He said, "Shame on you, somebody certainly did."

I said, "Who do you mean?"

He looked at me and said, "I mean the Lord Jesus Christ. He didn't *offer* to die; He did it!"

Why was the Lord Jesus willing to die? Just because He loved me and because He loved you. Friends, I don't care how orthodox you may be in your theology. I don't care who your father or mother or grandmother or grandfather may be, nor who you are. The Word of God says, "You must be born again." How? Through the death of Jesus Christ, by a simple act of faith as you receive Him as your Lord and Saviour. I'll illustrate it to you:

Out in Colorado Springs a couple of years ago, there was a freckle-faced elevator boy. He was one swell kid, but he wasn't saved. There was another one who was, and one day he said to me, "I wish you would talk to my friend. I've been trying to lead him to the Lord."

One day when I met him, I said, "Tell me something. Are you saved?"

He said, "I don't know."

I said, "You're not."

"What do you mean?"

I said, "If you were, you'd know. If somebody stepped up to me and asked me if I was an American and I said, 'I don't know,' they would take me to jail or to the cuckoo house. Fella, if you don't know whether or not you're saved, then you're not."

"You know," he said, "it has never quite clicked with me. I don't quite get it."

I said, "Do you believe that Jesus Christ died?"

"I've been taught that."

I asked, "Did you ever receive Christ?"

— 76 —

He answered, "That's just what I don't understand. How do you do that?"

I said, "Let me ask you something. Would you like to have a quarter?"

"Sure."

I said, "What do you have to do to get it?"

"I don't know."

"Well, if that's the case, I'll tell you," I said. "I'll give it to you as a gift. Now what?"

"I suppose I take it," he said.

He took the quarter, and I said, "Whose is it now?"

"It's mine unless you're a liar."

I said, "That's right. That's absolutely right. Now I want to show you something. I gave you a quarter and you took it and it's yours now. God gave you Jesus Christ, salvation, and everlasting life. To get the quarter you took it from my hand. To get Jesus Christ, you take it just like you did the quarter, but from the hand of God. Will you do it?"

And I could see his face light up as he looked at me and said, "Yes sir."

I said, "Tell me something, Bud. To whom does Jesus Christ belong?"

I can see him as he said, "He's mine."

Young folks, is He yours? Have you really been born again? Or are you hiding a heart full of sin behind the cloak of a lot of Scripture verses and other things? I wonder if God took you right now, if you are sure that you would go to Heaven? If you are not, make sure tonight.

THREE THINGS THAT NEED TO BE SETTLED

Message delivered by Rev. Robert Cook,
Associate Pastor, Midwest Bible Church, Chicago,
Saturday, August 5, 1944

I want you to think with me tonight about some verses from the twenty-first chapter of Luke. "Settle it therefore in your hearts, not to mediate before what ye shall answer: For I will give you a mouth and wisdom, which all your adversaries shall not be able to gainsay nor resist" (Luke 21:14, 15).

There are some decisions that may be put off—whether to go downtown today or tomorrow, whether to wear your red hat or your green one, and you, gentlemen, whether to wear your green tie or your yellow one with your brown suit. These are all unimportant decisions, but there are certain matters that can *never* be postponed. In fact, no life is effective until some decisions have been made. All of life is dependent upon certain things that need to be settled.

It is the admonition of our text that stirs my heart this evening: "Settle it therefore in your hearts." The authority of God's Word must be settled.

The reality of the message of the Cross must be settled. The Lordship and leadership of the Holy Ghost must be settled.

If I asked my audience how many really believe the Bible, I think almost all of you would say, "Yes, I believe the Bible from cover to cover. My parents had it in our home, and I was brought up to recognize the Bible as a holy and important book." You would probably say that your parents read to you from that Book, that you were trained to memorize certain Scripture passages, and that you have a very important place in your thinking for the Bible. I'm willing to admit that ninety-nine and forty-four one hundredths percent of our audience believes in the Bible. Still—I wonder whether you have ever settled in your heart the authority of the Word of God.

There are many people who believe in documents without believing in the authority of the document. For instance, here's a youngster who sees a cool, inviting pool of water. Before you can say, "Jack Robinson" this youngster is out of his clothes and into the water, enjoying a dip in the old swimming hole. In he goes, oblivious of the fact that there's a sign above him, a document that says, "No Swimming Allowed."

Now let us suppose that he sees a very imposing character coming over the brow of the hill, a man with shiny brass buttons on his coat, and all the marks of an officer of the law. My, isn't it wonderful what respect he has for *that* sign all of a sudden!

He believes in the authority of the sign—now! He believes that it means what it says. He puts his shirt over one arm and his stockings over the other, drapes his trousers over his shoulders and his shoes around his neck, hanging by their laces, and—all you can see is a cloud of dust. He got respect for the authority of that sign when he saw the person who could back it up.

I want to tell you that although you say, "I believe in the Bible and I'm trying to obey it," you really don't believe it or you would actually be obeying it.

A friend of mine some time ago said, "You say you believe God's Word," and then he asked me a very disturbing question. He said, "Just what part of the Bible did you believe today? You know, the Bible is full of promises. Just *what* did you believe today?"

I began to scratch my head and tried to think fast and my face got red. Here I was, a preacher—we are supposed to be super-holy!—and he was embarrassing me in front of people. I really hadn't believed any part of the Bible that day because I hadn't gotten down to business with God and decided what His Word had to say—to me! I had to make it part of my life, and then it carried some authority. My friends, until you settle the authority of God's Word, you will continue to flounder.

You say, "I'm interested in science." So am I, but did you ever check up on what the science books of a decade or so ago had to say? Back in nineteen hundred and . . . none of your business, I can remember some of the arguments I had with the science teacher. She did the best she could with what she had to work on, but I remember it was a rather feeble business. Whenever she said something I didn't quite agree with, I said, "The Word of God says so and so." She said, "Don't you realize that this is a scientific age and the Bible is antiquated and out-worn." You ought to believe science." We argued back and forth and finally compromised on a "C" average.

Today, if you go back and look at the science books we used back there, they just aren't up to date. As a matter of fact, some years ago I was going to sell some of my books. I took them to O'Leary's Book Store. (They take all the books that people want to sell when they are broke.) So I too them all down to O'Leary's and spread them out—a whole cardboard carton of them. Here was a literature book and a mathematics book. Here was the science book and a number of others.

The man said, "I'll take the mathematics book; that's still the same. You can take your literature book home, Sonny. It looks nice, and it has never been used. You can take your science book back, too."

I said, "Now listen, that was a good science book. I had to work hard to get a C average."

He said, "Yes, but you know, we don't believe the same things now." It wasn't many years ago *then,* and they don't believe the same things *now* that they believed *then* when they believed what they didn't believe when I went to school!

Can you beat it?

Yet they have the audacity to tell you that you're crazy and the Bible is old stuff because we have "science" today. But what can you do with science? Can science still the aching of your soul? Can you pillow your dying head upon the changing trends of science? Can you go to Heaven upon the wings of the Pythagorean Theorem? Can you do anything about your eternal destiny with a geometric proposition? No, you can't!

Tonight will you say, "O, God, I do believe Thy Word, and I'm going to take it seriously from now on—not simply carry it to a meeting and take someone else's word that it is the message of the Almighty without ever proving and living it. Right now, I'll settle the authority of the Word of God."

Another thing that needs to be settled is the reality of the message of the Cross. The same word translated "settle" in Luke 21:14 is translated in Luke 9:44 "sink down." "Let these sayings sink down." In other words, "Settle these sayings, for the Son of man shall be delivered into the hands of men." Jesus Christ was saying, "You better settle this matter about the crucifixion."

Let me ask you a question: What one factor contributed more to the confusion and disturbance of the disciples in the days immediately before and after the crucifixion than anything else? I think you will agree with me when I say that they *didn't really believe* He would be crucified and rise again. In other words, they had not settled the necessity for the message of the Cross in their hearts. What was it that the Lord said that day as He met those two disciples on the road to Emmaus? He said, "Why are you so sad?" They said, "Don't you know? Are you a stranger in town? They have crucified Jesus of Nazareth, and he was to redeem Israel." Then Jesus said to them, "O fools, and slow of heart to believe what the prophets have spoken: Ought not Christ to have suffered these things, and to enter into his glory?"

Much of the uncertainty that possesses people is traceable to the fact that they have never become absolutely sure that the message of the Cross is a necessity—for them! They know the story of the Cross—that Jesus died and was buried and rose again—but the reaction is very much like what I used to get some years ago when I would knock on the doors and tell the story of the Cross to folk on the West side of Chicago. I would begin to talk to them and tell them all about the Lord Jesus Christ. The response was almost always the same: "Ya, ya, ya"—BANG!—and the door was closed in my face. In other words, "Yes, I know all about it. Why are you bothering me with it? Get going!"

So many people are floundering because they have never come to the place of realizing that Jesus Christ had to die for *them*. If there had been no one else in all the universe but you, He would have died for *you,* because it was in the eternal purpose of God, and His purposes are carried out.

When you really understand the importance of the message of the Cross, you will be saying as Paul, "Christ Jesus came into the world to save sinners: *of whom I am chief."* When you have come far enough to do some real business with God, it will seem to you as though the whole universe had faded away and you stand in the presence of a Holy God as the greatest sinner of them all.

Do you remember the day you asked the Lord Jesus to come into your heart? You seemed to be the greatest sinner in all the world at that time. You need to settle tonight, my dear friends, the necessity of the message of a crucified Christ, not as a religious dogma, not as a doctrinal creed, not as a religious tenet to which you adhere, nor simply the basis of some religious relic you wear. You need to settle the fact that you *personally* needed to have a Saviour die for you, and that Jesus is that Saviour. I say frankly that a lot of people don't believe that. If you really believed it, you would already have received Jesus Christ as your Saviour. Have you settled that question?

The next thing you need to settle is the leadership and lordship of the Holy Spirit. The word translated "settle" in Luke 21, and "sink down" in Luke 9, is translated for us in Acts 19:21 as "purposed." "After these things were ended, Paul purposed in the spirit, when he had passed through Macedonia and Achaia, to go to Jerusalem, saying, After I have been there, I must also see Rome." He purposed where? In the Spirit. What Spirit? The Holy Spirit of God. Settle this thing in your heart, beloved! Not only the authority of the Word of God, and the necessity of salvation through faith in Jesus Christ, but now the leadership and lordship of the Holy Spirit of God.

You say, "Why bring that in here?" I'll tell you why: Because you must realize that only when the Holy Spirit is working in a life, does that life count for eternity. For instance, the beginning of salvation is brought about by the Holy Spirit. He does the convicting. "When he (the Spirit) is come, he will reprove the world of sin . . ." The very first pangs of suffering in your own conscience when you realized you were a sinner—who brought them there? Not the preaching, not the pleading, not the praying, but the working of the Holy Spirit of God. The work of regeneration when you are born again is the work of the Holy Spirit. Jesus said, "Except a man be born of water and of the Spirit, he cannot enter into the kingdom of God." The Holy Spirit actually brings you into the position of becoming a child of God, and after you are saved, the Holy Spirit tells you so. I never tell anyone that he is saved, because that is the work of the Holy Ghost (Rom. 8:16). If you are not sure you are saved, you ought to ask the Lord to make you sure. Then if you trust Him, the Holy Spirit will give you assurance because the Bible plainly says, "The Spirit itself beareth witness with our spirit, that we are the children of God."

The Holy Spirit helps you pray. Did you ever feel that you couldn't pray? Then perhaps you went to the Word (Rom. 8:26) and got a real background of Scripture and out from your heart came a real petition to God. The Spirit of God helped you pray.

The Holy Spirit leads people into service. "Ye shall receive power, after that the Holy Ghost is come upon you: and ye shall be witnesses unto me both in Jerusalem, and in all Judea, and in Samaria, and unto the uttermost part of the earth." The lordship and the leadership of the Holy Spirit—you need to settle that tonight.

A man whom I love in the things of the Lord told me that for years he was very active in Christian work. There was a period of several years during which he was preaching whenever he had opportunity. He gave out thousands of tracts and tried to do his best, but he told me rather ruefully that he could show very little evidence that anybody had ever been saved as a result of his hard work during that time.

Then one day he decided that there was something wrong with his approach. He got on his knees with his Bible and opened it to Romans 12:1 where it says, "I beseech you therefore, brethren, by the mercies of God, that ye present your bodies a living sacrifice, holy, acceptable unto God, which is your reasonable service." Somehow he saw the verse in a new light and said, "O, God, I've never done it before, but just now I do give my body and all that I am to Thee. Work through me, blessed Holy Spirit."

He went downstairs and said to his wife, "I've done something I never did before. I gave my body to the Holy Spirit, and I expect He's going to use me. I'm going to call you up as soon as I've won the first soul."

He went to work that morning with real victory: About ten o'clock the telephone rang. His wife answered and heard him say, "I just won two souls that the Lord sent in to me!" I wonder what happened? You know. He had settled the lordship and leadership of the Holy Spirit in his life.

Will you settle these things? First of all, whether you really believe the Bible is true: then settle whether or not you really believe you need Jesus, the crucified Christ; and, Christian friends, you settle the matter of whether or not the Holy Spirit has the use of your body—all of it.

Listen to our text again: "Settle it therefore in your hearts."

FIVE WORDS

Message delivered by Dr. Harry Rimmer,
Author and Lecturer, Los Angeles, Calif.,
September 2, 1944

The trouble with average Christian young people is that their mentality is like a disorderly house. They have no pegs whereupon to drape the garments of their thinking. They have no basic philosophy of Christianity. Tonight, in twenty minutes I have the impossible task of giving you that basic philosophy so that you will know *what* is a Christian, and *why* is a Christian, and *how* you can be saved. I'm going to give you an outline and let you build it up for yourselves. I'm going to drive five pegs into the wall of your mentality and let you hang your own thoughts upon those five pegs. The five pegs are five words, and in those five words are encompassed the whole horizon of God's dealings with man.

My first word, of course, if I'm going to be basically accurate, I take out of the first chapter of Genesis. Not only is that the foundation of belief, but it is also the most complete revelation of God we have anywhere in sacred literature. In the first chapter I find my first word, and that is *creation*. "And God said, Let us make man in our image, after our likeness: and let them have dominion over the fish of the sea, and over the fowl of the air, and over the cattle, and over all the earth, and over every creeping thing that creepeth upon the earth. So God created man in his own image, in the image of God created he him; male and female created he them."

If you are to have a basic philosophy of Christianity, you have to begin with the word *creation*. Without that you have no place to start. This word "creation" means to call into existence that which never had any form of existence before. Some people say that they believe in creation and evolution. That's just like trying to ride two horses that are going in different directions. The theory of evolution has man going one way and the theory of creation has him going the opposite way. When *man* tells the story of man, he starts it as low down as he can conceive, and then brags him as high as he can.

Do you know how the theory of evolution began? Let me boil it down and give it to you in a few words. In college the professor begins by saying, "Once upon a time a long time ago there was a little one-celled creature tossed upon the shore in some queer way. Instead of dying, this little creature lay right down and thought it over. Deciding that it was nicer to live on the ground rather than in the water, he began a process of development that is the most fabulous thing man has ever conceived. He decided that in order to get around he needed some legs, so he sprouted a pair. But he didn't get along on one pair of legs very well, so he got another pair. Then one day one of his enemies chased him up a tree."

"Where does the enemy come from?" I ask.

The professor yells, "Shut up!" and goes on.

"Then one day this little fellow made a startling discovery. He found that he had a tail that he could hang by. But one night a sudden wind blew up and before he realized what was happening, he landed on his ear. He stood up on his hind legs, and he's been that way ever since."

This is a brief condensation of the theory of evolution. I'm merely pointing out that they have man consistently going up. He starts in insignificance and he develops gradually until he is the creature that you see him now, and according to that, if man ever fell, he fell up. That's a good trick if you can do it.

The theory of creation says that God created man perfectly. God made man in the image and likeness of himself, but man stooped to sin until he was lower than the beasts of the field. I mean that literally. There is no animal that has to plead guilty to the awful indictment against the human race. And when man had fallen to be lower than animals, he never rose again until Christ came and lifted him out of his sin. When you start your basic philosophy of Christianity, my friend, you have to start somewhere, and since the theory of evolution has been utterly discredited and repudiated, and the theory of creation is the only thing left, you have to begin with the word *creation*.

Our second word is also from the book of Genesis, in the fifth chapter, the word *generation*. "And Adam lived an hundred and thirty years, and begat a son in his own likeness, after his image; and called his name Seth." It is not stated in the Scripture that any of us are born in the likeness of God. Adam was created in God's image, but we are born in the image and likeness of Adam. You say, "If Adam was created in God's image, what's the difference?" There is a vital difference. After Adam had sinned and fallen and had become the sin-ruined image and likeness of God, the generations that followed had a fallen nature. Those things that I determine to do, I catch myself never doing, and those things I swear I ought not to do, I do— I have a fallen nature. I have three strikes on me when I am born. I have no chance to succeed morally. I inherited from a long line of sinful ancestors a disposition to sin.

But if that is all I had to say, I never would have come. I have a third word from the eighth chapter of Romans. "For as many as are led by the Spirit of God, they are the sons of God . . . ye have received the Spirit of adoption, whereby we cry, Abba, Father." Here we have the word *adoption*. As many as are led, they are the sons of God. How about those that are not led? Obviously they are not the sons of God. All men are the children of Adam, but they have to be adopted into the family of God before they are his sons.

In my family we have three children, mine by right of birth. We always wanted four, and so we thought of adopting the fourth. There was a little fellow by the name of Thomas Kelly who spent a lot of time at our house. He didn't have a dad and so we thought very seriously of adopting him, and we would have were it not for a lot of legal impediments. If I had gone into court and adopted him according to the law, he would have come out with the name of Thomas Rimmer instead of Thomas Kelly. He would have come to my house and lived with me, and according to the laws of the state of California, he would be my son by adoption. When I died, if I left no will, the law would divide my estate equally among the four boys. He would have every right as a natural son. Therefore, when we are adopted by

God, we become heirs of God, and joint heirs with Jesus Christ. If I am adopted into the family of God, then, I have every right that Jesus has with the Father. That's a magnificent vista open to me, but I won't stop to enlarge on it.

There is one thing wrong with adoption. It doesn't change the nature of the individual. If I had adopted Thomas Kelly, his name would be changed to Rimmer, but as long as he lived there would be Kelly thoughts. He would have a Kelly heart and Kelly blood. He would have a Kelly nature until he died.

Here is God's difficulty. He is not willing to adopt the fallen children of Adam and leave them with an Adam nature. So we have to have a new word, and that word is *regeneration*. John 3:7 says, "Marvel not that I said unto thee, Ye must be born again." Jesus never said you ought to be born again. Jesus never said it's a grand experience you ought to have. He never said other people have enjoyed it, why don't you try it. If you will let me put that verse of the third chapter of John into the vernacular of the day, this is what He said: "Marvel not that I say unto you, you have got to be born again." When you are born again by the act of the Holy Ghost and the convicting power of the Word of God, there is formed in you a new nature, and the nature of Almighty God replaces the nature of Adam in you.

That brings me to my fifth word which comes from the verse which is my life motto: II Corinthians 5:17. "If any man be in Christ, he is a new creature: old things are passed away; behold, all things are become new." That's the verse that the preacher used on the night that I was saved. He wasn't much of a preacher, and it wasn't much of a meeting. I was walking up a street in San Francisco and a crowd of young people were holding a street meeting. The meeting was practically a failure; I was the only one saved. But as far as I was concerned, it was the greatest evangelistic campaign ever held at any time.

Now here's my word, and that word is *consummation*. "If any man be in Christ . . . old things are passed away." Translated from the Greek it reads, "All things are in the process of becoming new." When you take Christ, never forget that there is a work continuing in you which never stops until you behold your Saviour.

I would like you to see that this new nature is not the old Adam nature fixed up so it will run a few years longer. God isn't in the junk business.

Years ago I formed the habit of stealing my two sons from their mother and taking them on a fishing trip. One day my wife said to me, "Did you ever stop to think about how selfish you are? You take the car and leave me to get around the best way I can."

I said, "That's right." The next morning I went to a used car dealer and bought a second hand Ford to go fishing with, and I paid forty-five dollars for it. When we bought that thing, it ran. All you had to do was to keep putting in gas and water. When we said we were going two hundred miles and back in the thing, my wife laughed and said, "I bet an apple pie against a box of candy it won't run a block."

We started out and it went two miles before anything happened. We got out and fixed it and went four miles more. We landed in San Francisco and found we had a broken landing gear. Finally that was fixed and we went merrily on our way.

It only broke four times on the way coming home. When we finally got that thing home on two cylinders and everybody pushing I said, "Phooey, I'll never try that again!" My wife played a mean trick on the colored boy. She sold it to him for fifteen dollars. That was the first time I ever bought a heap of junk, and that's the last time I ever will. I'm through trying to make a pile of junk run.

God feels that way about the Adam nature in you. When I came to Jesus Christ, Almighty God just put a new motor in me, and it's been running ever since, a streamlined job if you ever saw one!

This is what I'm trying to say. God wants to make out of you a complete new machine. I—that's the old Adam nature—am crucified with Christ. What is a Christian? Paul says, "It is 'Christ in you the hope of glory.'" What is a Christian? An ordinary human being like you and me into whom Jesus Christ has come to take up residence in the person of the Holy Spirit.

When you take Christ, He comes in and resides in you from that minute on. You remember what is written in the third chapter of the book of Ephesians. "That Christ may dwell in your hearts by faith; that ye, being rooted and grounded in love." Let me close with this one verse from Ephesians 2:10, "For we are his workmanship, created in Christ Jesus unto good works, which God hath before ordained that we should walk in them." Let me give you just one more passage—Colossians 3:9, 10: "Lie not one to another, seeing that ye have put off the old man with his deeds; and have put on the new man, which is renewed in knowledge after the image of him that created him."

We have completed the cycle. We began with creation. God created man in God's image and likeness. Man fell, but fallen man may be adopted into the family of God on condition that he will be born again and get a new nature which makes of him a child of God.

Are you a Christian? When we say, "Take Christ as your Saviour" do you know what we are trying to offer you? He'll blot out every sin against your record. You'll receive a new nature, and He'll give you victory day by day. There is no reason why you should be defeated. Take Christ as your Saviour and your present life is transformed.

That's the basic philosophy of Christianity. Do you know how to get this? He said, "Whosoever therefore shall confess me before men, him will I confess also before my Father which is in heaven." The Holy Spirit led Paul to write these words: "That if thou shalt confess with thy mouth the Lord Jesus, and shalt believe in thine heart that God hath raised him from the dead, thou shalt be saved."

If you want to be born again and become a child of God with present victory and future assurance, I'll tell you how. Just lift your heart right now and say, "I here and now take Christ as my Saviour. I surrender my life to him, and with the help of God, I'll live my life for Him from now on." That's all you need to do.

"Thou Art My Hiding Place"

Message delivered by Dr. H. A. Ironside,
Pastor, Moody Memorial Church, Chicago,
Saturday, September 16, 1944

Psalm 32:7, "Thou art my hiding place; thou shalt preserve me from trouble; thou shalt compass me about with songs of deliverance."

In the early part of this Psalm we find a man hiding *from* God, and then when we get down to the seventh verse, we find him hiding *in* God. I wonder whether there are any here tonight who are trying to hide from God? I wonder whether there are any who have been pursued by God in His loving kindness and grace throughout the years, and yet you have been trying to get away from Him, where you wouldn't hear His voice . . . you're trying to silence the voice of your own conscience, and giving yourself to indulgence in things you know in your own heart are ruinous both to your soul and body—trying to find a hiding place from God.

That was David's condition. He had sinned—sinned terribly. Sinned so that to the present day, though three thousand years have rolled by, scoffers still smile as they talk of David, the man after God's own heart, and the awful sin into which he fell. If they only knew how broken hearted he was because of his sin! Think of him bowing before God and crying out, "Against thee, thee only, have I sinned, and done this evil." If they would follow him into the sanctuary of the Lord, where he prayed, "Thou desirest not sacrifice, else would I give it."

It was as if he said, "There is no sacrifice that man could offer that could ever atone for the sin that has marred my testimony and scarred my life." "Purge me... and I shall be clean; wash me, and I shall be whiter than snow."

Yes, David sinned, and he tried for a whole year to keep his sin to himself. He says in this Psalm, "When I kept silence, my bones waxed old through my roaring all the day long, For day and night thy hand was heavy upon me: my moisture is turned into the drought of summer."

There is nothing that will take away the joy of living like unconfessed sin. A person with a guilty conscience is the most miserable person. Of course, it is possible to fall so deeply into sin that the conscience at last will fail to register, and so we read in God's Word of some whose hearts are so hardened that they have no feeling and they no longer think anything of the depths of iniquity into which they have plunged.

Young man, young woman, be thankful if you still have a conscience that makes you unhappy when you sin against God. David's conscience was like that, and though he tried to keep from confessing it and didn't want to come face to face with God about his sin, yet he was miserable and wretched in hiding from God. Then, at last when he couldn't stand it any longer, he says, "I acknowledged my sin unto thee, and mine iniquity have I not hid. I said, I will confess my transgressions unto the Lord; and thou forgavest the iniquity of my sin." And so he could exclaim, "Blessed is he whose transgression is forgiven, whose sin is covered."

Now David lived a thousand years before the Lord Jesus Christ came into the world, and yet his sin was dealt with at the Cross of Calvary. It was because of what Christ was yet to do that God was able to send the message through Nathan, the prophet: "The Lord also hath put away thy sin."

Probably many of you have heard the story of the little Scotch lad. He was what the Scotch called "dull." This wee little laddie used to go to the kirk and listen to the great sermons. There were many that he couldn't understand very well. There were so many of the "Aurora Borealis" type of sermons that were away up in the air. The only thing he got of these great sermons was this, that away up somewhere beyond the stars, beyond the clouds, beyond the sun and moon, there was a terrible being that they called God. He had awful eyes that look right through the heavens. They could see in the dark, eyes that could look into the heart and could see every known thing that everyone ever did, and every thought that anyone ever thought, and someday this God was going to call everybody to account for all the wrong things done.

It used to stir the heart of little Jack, the Scotch laddie. He would walk up and down wringing his hands and saying, "I'm so afeared of God. Oh, I dinna want to meet Him. I wish I could run away from Him." People tried to explain to Jack that after all God might have mercy on a poor laddie. One day he went to the kirk and the great preacher was not there. Only a lay-man, a humble elder was there. He stood in front of the Lord's table and in a very simple way he spoke from the most wonderful of all texts, John 3:16, "For God so loved the world that he gave his only begotten Son, that whosoever believeth in him should not perish, but have everlasting life." He made it all so clear about why Jesus came and why He died on the cross. Why He shed His precious blood that we might be free, that guilty men and women and boys and girls might be forgiven and accepted of God. It all went straight to little Jack's heart, and he bowed his head and was thanking God for his wonderful Christ.

He didn't notice that all the people had left and he was there alone, save for the sexton. Finally the sexton said, "Come my little lad, it's time for you to be gang home noo."

He looked up and with a wonderful smile said, "Do ye ken, I'm no afeared of God, noo."

The sexton said, "You've been a bad laddie and you may well be afeared."

Little Jack replied, "Yes, I've sinned, but my sins have all been blotted out and I'm noo afeared of God noo, I'm gang to heaven."

The sexton said, "Explain yourself."

Jack scratched his poor addled pate and said, "Some day little John will see a great big white desk and on the desk He'll hae a great big Bible book with the names of everbody who ever lived and all the sins they have ever done. And when little John comes up before God, he'll turn to the big Bible book and find the page with John's name at the top and Jesus Christ will be there with his bleeding hand and put it down quick. God will say, 'I canna find a sin here. Let little John gang into heaven!'"

Little John's theology was pretty accurate. Come to God here and now for "He is faithful and just to forgive your sins," and "The blood of Jesus Christ cleanseth us from all sin."

So David, having put his trust in the promises of God and relying upon the pledge that God had given of the One coming, said with confidence, "Thou art my hiding place." Can you say that? He's not hiding from God any more—he's hiding in God.

My eldest son taught me a lesson when he was a wee lad. He was six years old before his brother came, and a lonely kind of a fellow for his father was away a great deal. When he would come home, he would have to try to be a big brother to his little son. He liked to play bear better than anything. Did you ever play bear? This is the way we played it. I was the bear and I would have to get down on all fours and my job was to growl.

The little fellow would come into the room as though he didn't know there was a bear there, and suddenly the bear would come rushing out of his den and the little fellow would run from room to room. The rule was that I had to keep down on all fours. That boy certainly could run and it was rather hard for a heavy old bear to catch a lively youngster.

We would go through one room after another, and finally he ran into the kitchen and found himself in a corner. It wouldn't open up to let him through, and there was that bear! The bear was actually upon him, and he was scared and alarmed. You know how real those things are to children. Suddenly just before the bear caught him, he wheeled around and caught his breath and said, "You're not a bear at all, you're just my own father!" and he jumped into my arms.

Then I thought that's just the way I was. I was running away from God. And one never-to-be-forgotten night in my soul's history, I ran right into a corner where, convicted of sin at last through the guidance of the Holy Spirit, I turned to the One who was pursuing me, and said as I turned, "Oh, God, you're not my enemy, but my loving, tender Father." Instead of running away from Him, I ran *to* Him and found a hiding place in Him.

> Rock of Ages, cleft for me,
> Let me hide myself in Thee;
> Let the water and the blood,
> From thy wounded side which flowed,
> Be of sin the double cure,
> Save from wrath and make me pure.

So tonight my soul can say, "Thou art my hiding place; thou shalt preserve me from trouble; thou shalt compass me about with songs of deliverance."

Do you know that Hiding Place from the storms of life and the covert from temptations that come your way? That hiding place is the Lord Jesus Christ. Will you come to Him tonight?

"CHICAGOLAND YOUTH FOR CHRIST"

Torrey M. Johnson, Director   Douglas Fisher, Managing Director

ADVISORY COUNCIL

Sten Benson
Walter Block
Freelin A. Carlton
Einar A. Comfield
Al J. Conn
Robert A. Cook

Howard Duntz
William Erny
Douglas Fisher
Floyd E. Gephart
Joseph Gunderson
Clifton B. Hedstrom

Torrey M. Johnson
Enoch J. Malmstrom
Henry Riemersma
Charles F. Stein
H. J. Taylor
Robert Van Kampen

THE BUSINESS WORLD

Ernest Alder
Roy E. Anderson
Roy Baumann
J. Paul Bennett, M.D.
Harold O. Benson
Stanley M. Berntson
Peter M. Black
Charles E. Bodeen
Kenneth J. Brouwer
Judith B. Carlson
LaVerne Carlson
Bruce E. Cederoth
Einar Christianssen
George Christophersen
Ardith M. Cornelius
Victor E. Cory
Stuart Crippen
Carl A. Dahlin
U. S. Deahl, Jr.
Clyde H. Dennis

Erling A. Dunhom
T. Wesley Eyres
Carl J. Frizen
William Garland
Audrey Gerken
William Gray
Carl A. Gundersen
Lacy Hall
Arthur Hansen
V. C. Hogren
Andrew H. Jessen
J. Martin Johnson
Mae Johnson
Ivan Lageschulte
Mel Larsen
Ferne Larson
Reamer G. Loomis
Mrs. Robert C. Loveless
Elmer Matthews
Mrs. George S. May
Blair Meeker

H. D. Mielke
Mabel Moore
Mrs. Donald M. Nelson
Chas. Palmquist, Sr.
E. Reeby
Theis Reynertson
Chester C. Scholl
R. Hugh Seffens
Beverly Shea
Mark C. Spencer, D.D.S.
Evelyn Stenbeck
A. J. Susans
Kenneth N. Taylor
Roy A. Thompson
Arnold Torsell
Cornelius J. Ulrich
Charles Warner
Helen Warner
Robert William Wyatt
Andrew Wyzenbeek

ORGANIZATIONAL LEADERS

Alvera Anderson, President, Chicago Christian Nurses' Fellowship

Amy Anderson, Chairman, Christian Business Girls' Association

Thelma Barnett, Secretary, Fox Valley Young People's Bible Fellowship

Sten W. Benson, Chairman, Northwest Gospel Fellowship

Nancy Carpenter, Chmn., Christian Business and Professional Women

Harry B. Cork, President, Chicago Camp, The Gideons

Peter Deyneka, Director, Russian Gospel Association

C. V. Egemeier, Executive Secretary, Greater Chicago Sunday School Association

Christian L. Eicher, Secretary, World Wide Prayer and Missionary Union

William Graham, Director, Suburban Men's Fellowship

Mrs. William Gray, President, Gideon Women's Auxiliary

Walter F. Hanselman, President, Christian Teachers' Fellowship

Kenneth Hansen, The Brigades

Olena Mae Hendrickson, Chicago Child Evangelism Fellowship

Maj. Dallas P. Leader, Terr. Y. P. Secretary, The Salvation Army

G. A. Lundmark, President, Pentecostal Young People's Fellowship

June Lundquist, Secretary, Miracle Book Club

Dorothy Marx, President, South District, Baptist Youth Fellowship

Eleanor Nerhus, Methodist Youth Fellowship

Edward Thoraldsen, Commander of Aaron Post No. 788, American Legion

Arnie Olsen, Luther League

Anna Penn, President, Chicago Christian Endeavor

Dora Reid, Executive Secretary, Christian Teachers' Fellowship

Elmer Sandberg, President, Free Church Youth Fellowship

Vaughn Shoemaker, Chairman, Gospel Fellowship Club

Lois Thiessen, President, Pioneer Girls

Dr. M. E. Wadsworth, Director, Great Commission Prayer League

Stacey Woods, Inter-Varsity Christian Fellowship

CPSIA information can be obtained at www.ICGtesting.com
Printed in the USA
BVOW03s2359091014

370282BV00020B/194/P

9 781162 761701